SuperPuppy®
Training Manual

How to Teach the Best Puppy Training Class You've Ever Had!

By Peter J. Vollmer and Nancy Vollmer

Illustrated by Nancy Vollmer and Andrea Myklebust
Edited by Kathy Mahoney
v 2.1

TABLE OF CONTENTS

HOMEWORK HANDOUTS

" WALDO "

INTRODUCTION

It's been my dream to help change the way our family pet dogs are raised. For more than a decade I've been assisting pet owners with their dog behavior problems. After listening to their complaints, discovering how they raise their puppies, and how they deal with their pets' problems, one fact rings out loud and clear: American pet owners have no idea of how canines develop socially, emotionally, and mentally into confident, outgoing, respectful, well-behaved, well-balanced adults! It's my view that this lack of understanding is the *single most* important reason that over 65% of all dogs are not with their original owners, only 15% of dog owners report positively about their owner/pet relationship, and one dog is "put down" every four seconds for nonmedical reasons!

New Knowledge

If we were still living in the first half of this century, I could better understand the reasons for this unfortunate failure rate. The necessary research to further our knowledge of canine social development had not been done. But starting with the work of Scott, Fuller, and Hebb in the 1940's and continuing with the wolf studies of Allen, Mech, Fox, and others in the 1950's, 1960's, and 1970's, we began to see how these marvelous creatures develop socially into functioning pack members. Since then, many other pieces of the puzzle have been put into place. We now know more about puppy social and mental development than we know about infant development! It seems to me our next step should be to inform as many new pet owners as possible about what we know!

Working Together

This is where you come in. If every veterinary clinic, humane society, and training organization in this country included a class especially designed for people with dogs between three and six months of age, I have no doubt that we could *immediately* begin turning around the enormous failure rate!

All Purpose Class

There's another advantage in having a well-structured, well-run puppy training class: Conformation and Obedience exhibitors can begin preparing their dogs for competition much earlier than thought possible. Because a SuperPuppy Class concentrates on promoting those basic skills ALL dogs need in order to compete effectively, the same class can be used to prepare for both!

Confidence to perform under new and challenging conditions, attentiveness to the task at hand, trust and respect, as well as affection, for their owners and handlers, are qualities shared by most true winners.

If you're interested in hunting, herding, search and rescue, tracking and trailing, lure coursing, Schutzhund, or any other of the wide variety of training avenues, laying down the necessary foundation can and should be done as early as possible. A SuperPuppy Class meets all of these needs, and, unlike many Basic Obedience classes, is *a heck of a lot of fun!*

Careful Preparation

The purpose of this manual is to show how a class for owners of very young dogs can be structured. Starting early may be a great idea, but it also requires careful planing and preparation. We all know young puppies are highly impressionable. Since their early experiences can have a powerful influence on their adult attitudes, great care must be taken to provide a richly positive, rewarding experience. We also know how difficult and frustrating teaching novice pet owners can be. Concentrating on how two-footed adults best learn new things is a major part of the SuperPuppy Class approach.

Everyone Benefits

Nancy and I tell all our new puppy students that the purpose of SuperPuppy Class is to teach them how to raise and train their dog not just to be an okay pet, but a great pet - the best dog they'll ever have!

We believe great dogs come from super puppies. We all know how important good breeding is if we're going to have a good dog; we now know how vitally important a well-bred dog's early experiences are if it's to achieve the potential its genetics have provided.

Time and time again we've seen average dogs of good temperament really "turn on" while in SuperPuppy Class. They begin to sparkle and shine as they become more polished and self-assured. Think what could happen to exceptionally well-bred pups!

We've also seen problem puppies change their behavior. They may never become great dogs, but in the eyes of their owners they become wonderful companions instead of heartaches. If their owners learn early how to manage them, these pups can grow up to live long, useful lives.

Super People

Even a well-structured, well-run SuperPuppy Class isn't for everyone. People are too complex for that. The people SuperPuppy Class will appeal to are those pet owners, trainers, and exhibitors who not only want the best possible dog they can have, but are willing to try something different, start early, and work hard to get it. Thank goodness there's an abundance of people like this around!

Once you put the word out that you have a new, exciting, training program for people with dogs *under* six months, they'll find you. Then all you have to do is deliver, and I'm going to do my very best to ensure that you can. I know it won't be easy for most of you to take a new view of training, but achieving anything worthwhile is seldom easy — and there are few other things in life as worthwhile as living with a great dog and helping others to do so as well!

BRIEF HISTORY

Puppy class was originally called Kindergarten Puppy Training or K.P.T.. By and large, K.P.T. was a socialization experience for young dogs. A few of the basic commands were introduced by holding the puppies into the "Sit," "Stand," "Down," and "Stay" positions.

Housebreaking and crate training were discussed, but little serious training was done. Much of the time was devoted to meeting and playing with other pups and their owners.

Because of the young dogs' short attention span and emotional immaturity, trainers felt the puppies needed to grow up before learning more complicated obedience commands.

Beginners' Basic Obedience

The model most often used to teach pet owners how to control their older dogs was developed from obedience competition training. Its original purpose was to prepare dogs older than six months for the Companion Dog (C.D.) degree.

After shot records and equipment are checked, a typical Beginners' Class starts with a brief introduction on how to use the leash and choke collar to influence the dogs' behavior.

Next, the instructor, sometimes with the help of assistants, explains and demonstrates a particular command. Typically these commands include "Heel," "Sit," "Down," "Stay," "Front," and "Finish". The class as a whole is asked to perform the demonstrated exercise. Assistant instructors try to help students who are having difficulty.

Corrective actions for nuisances such as "jumping up," "mouthing," and "barking" may also be demonstrated. Usually owners with more serious concerns such as aggression and extreme shyness are worked with individually.

A typical Beginners' Class meets weekly for ten sessions. If it's a good class, about one half of the starting students will graduate. Graduation usually consists of a judged, Sub-Novice type, performance. The pet owners are congratulated and given a nice token of achievement for their efforts.

SUPERPUPPY CLASS

Adult Education

SuperPuppy Class uses a remarkably different approach to training, and it's the training of the *people,* as well as the dogs, that's so different! As you know, most of your non-canine students will be adults. If you're going to teach adults successfully in a non-compulsory class, you must have a very clear idea of WHAT they want to learn and WHY they want to learn it, or they'll simply drop out!

If you were to teach an accounting course to junior bankers, you'd know that junior bankers want to learn basic accounting principles in order to compete more effectively on the job and make lots of money. This is straightforward and easily recognized.

What if you were teaching a course on tropical fish breeding? In this case the WHY may not be the same for everyone. Some students might want to learn how to breed and raise fish for competition; others might wish to have the best all-round aquarium setup on the block; still others are only interested in helping to create beautiful, healthy tropical fish for aesthetic reasons; someone else might want to breed and sell the fingerlings for profit. If you teach the class as if everyone wants to show in competition, you're going to have quite a few disappointed students.

Inaccurate Expectations

When we start talking about dog training classes, the reasons become even more obscure. Some people come to class because they want to do "something" with their dog, others because of competition goals, but most new pet owners come to basic obedience class because they're having some difficulty with Waldo. They want him to be better behaved, and they want *him* to learn to be better behaved by coming to class. Sounds straightforward — but is it really?

Right away there's a problem because the students' expectations are not accurate. Waldo, with the help of the trainers, will most likely learn to behave when he's at class. However, he's not learning *how* to behave, he's only learning *where* to behave. At home, it's up to Mom and Dad to teach Waldo *how* to behave by applying what they've learned at class.

Few first time students understand this! At class, it's primarily the *pet owners* who learn. New dog owners should come to class to learn *how to teach* their dogs. Then their dogs can learn to be better behaved!

Why Are They There?

Why do they want Waldo to be better behaved in the first place? I doubt it's because they want to put a C.D. on him. Most likely it's because if he doesn't shape up, he's NOT GOING TO BE AROUND!

As far as they're concerned, the problems aren't because of any lack of effort on their part. They've tried everything they can think of, and nothing has worked. They've used the tried and "true" remedies of the past, and they've probably tried the latest techniques picked up from friends, relatives, coworkers, and neighbors. Some of them have even gotten hold of a training book or two. But, one thing is clear: they're at Beginners' Obedience class because they're becoming very frustrated, and may be about to get rid of their dog.

Student Attitudes and Expectations

This is a very difficult teaching situation. Many of your students are taking class because it's the last hope they have of solving an emotionally charged problem. Their attitudes are somewhat less than positive, to say the least. Combine this with inaccurate expectations of what class is all about, and you're off to a very shaky start.

Now for the coup de grace. What is going to be taught to them is how to teach their dogs to "Heel," "Stay," "Down," "Front," and "Finish" while on leash! How this can possibly teach Waldo to stop harassing the mailman is a total mystery, not particularly clear, and a little beyond them.

They not only want Waldo to leave the mailman alone, but also to stop chasing their cat and the neighbors' cats; not bark at them when they're eating; stay off their laps when they're trying to read or watch TV; stop using the house like a cat uses its litter box; stop eating the patio furniture; stop tearing up the sofa when they leave the house; stop knocking Aunt Martha over when she visits; stop flying out the front door every time it's opened; stop trying to bite every kid on a skate-board; and stop nipping at their hands and clothes. They want Waldo to play gently, to listen when they say "No," and to come when called when it's time to take a bath or do something other than eat!

Starting Early

SuperPuppy Class gets around many of the problems and frustrations of Basic Obedience classes in several ways. By starting with people whose dogs haven't had months to perfect bad habits, you'll have students who come to class with more positive attitudes, and you'll have puppies who will be easier to retrain!

This is not to say they're not having real problems with their pups' behavior, but in most cases these problems haven't yet reached relationship-threatening proportions! Since the puppy is still cute, vulnerable, and malleable, most people aren't yet seriously reconsidering their decision to have a dog!

Setting the Goals

SuperPuppy Class specifically devotes one entire class, the Orientation meeting, to stating goals that are compatible with new pet owner needs. How these goals will be achieved is made crystal clear. "This is an adult education class. The primary purpose of the class is to teach you how to raise and train your dogs. This is how we're going to do it, and these are the reasons why we're doing things this way." Then, people with other views on what a puppy training class should be can either modify those views, or leave without any further obligation.

Homework

Another major difference between SuperPuppy Class and Basic Obedience class is that pet owners are expected to read about the subject. The *SuperPuppy* book, weekly handouts reviewing what was covered at class, and other pertinent reading material are assigned! At the Orientation it's made clear that commitment, study, and practice are necessary if they're to achieve their goals, and they're told they'll need to complete specific homework assignments.

A non-compulsory, adult education class can't really enforce a homework requirement. People can easily neglect assignments or drop out. If they neglect the assignments, they may be embarrassed by their performance at class. This embarrassment may lead to dropping out. If they drop out, the trade-off, in their minds, is losing the enrollment fee. How much of a sacrifice will that be?

We all know more is needed to get them working and keep them working, so embedded within the SuperPuppy Class structure are incentives and motivators to keep new pet owners enthusiastically involved in class.

Quick Success

What is really going to get them hooked on class is for them to become immediately successful in shaping up Waldo. This is the reason the first three weeks of SuperPuppy Class are devoted to those nagging, at-home behavior problems. We also begin talking about how to establish ways of managing the puppy that prevent other problems from developing.

Identifying Individual Differences

In most Basic classes, it's assumed at the outset, that the dogs have equal learning abilities. They should be able to learn at the same rate, so they're all taught the same thing, in the same way, at the same time. But, if they truly had similar abilities, an experienced trainer would be able to use the same methods to teach each dog and could expect to get the same results. We all know this isn't possible.

Furthermore, I don't know of any canine learning studies where the research groups showed little or no variability in measured performance, so it's only logical to conclude that the dogs in any training class will vary widely. Even puppies from the same litter can show remarkable differences in ability and temperament! Recognizing these differences and assigning puppies of like types to the same groups is an important reason behind SuperPuppy Class's success.

Teaching Groups

SuperPuppy Class is divided into Teaching Groups. Each instructor, or Group Leader, is assigned no more than eight puppies. The assignments are based on the dogs' age, size, abilities, and temperaments. When you put puppies of similar abilities and temperaments together, their owners can meet other people with similar concerns. All of a sudden they're no longer alone.

Shy puppies and their owners form the Bashful Group. Wanda's owners can discover that she isn't the odd wallflower they thought she was! In Group, she can take her time to meet puppies who are also reserved. There's no pressure put on her to say "hello." Once the ice is broken, it'll be much easier for her to meet new people and the other puppies.

Young Waldo and his pals form another Group — the Bold Group. The Waldo owners are shown how to manage their puppies when they meet other dogs and people. These owners are also grateful to know they're not alone, and can begin to share stories of "Waldo's" latest escapades.

First Three Weeks

During the first three class meetings, we teach how to use the leash as a training tool instead of a tether. New pet owners (NUPOs) learn that if they use the leash properly, their pups will quickly learn not to pull them around. (Conformation people can work on gaiting.) Once they've learned how to stop the pulling, we show them how to begin teaching the pups to follow whenever they change direction or pace. Next, we begin to show them how to teach their puppies to come when called using Front.

We also show them how to cut nails, clean teeth and ears, and introduce brushing. These are very useful skills for the pet owner to have, but the underlying reason for these topics is subordination.

Our feeling is if the puppy allows his owner to groom him without a struggle and without fear, he's saying something very positive about the relationship they're developing. Puppies must trust their owners. They must learn that their owners are powerful enough to prevent them from avoiding an uncomfortable, boring situation. They must learn respect for the owners' wishes, as *trust* and *respect*, as well as *affection* and *communication* are the key components of a healthy, sound dog/owner relationship.

If the owners are able to groom their puppies without a struggle, they really start to feel in control. During Orientation we take a great deal of time explaining that subordination is a natural, normal part of growing up for all canines. Unless the puppy is subordinate to its owner and all other able family members, its chances of becoming a super pet aren't that good.

Final Three Weeks

The last three SuperPuppy Class meetings are concerned with teaching NUPOs how to teach basic skills such as Drop, Wait, Front and Controlled Walking under intense distraction.

Usually there are plenty of distractions at any training class. But to make it even more challenging and *fun* as well, SuperPuppy Class introduces an obstacle course in Week Four and continues through with it to graduation. We use the obstacles as teaching aids because they are *tremendous* confidence-builders for both puppies and owners.

Young, healthy dogs are like little Olympians. They love to do athletic things! Obstacles give them that chance, while at the same time teach them to think. Many of the obstacles take careful, thorough preparation on everyone's part.

SuperPuppy Class uses tunnels, a teeter totter, inverted V-ramp, and several other obstacles. One goal is to teach the pup to Front on command through the tunnel and find the owner hiding behind a barrier one hundred feet away. If this isn't enough, after he leaves the tunnel the pup will have to run between two other puppies who are Waiting in Sits!*

SuperPuppy Class Graduation

Graduation isn't a mandatory, individually judged event. We feel it's a very important *teaching class* because people must put it "all together" at graduation.

The idea is for NUPOs to use *all* the new commands they've learned, as well as their new relationship, to teach their pups to negotiate an unfamiliar obstacle course while dragging the leash.

After we explain and demonstrate the course, we give them all the time they want to "practice." What we don't tell them is that "practice" is their final exam! Nancy and I watch and use an evaluation form to indicate their teaching strengths and areas needing improvement. Many people want to "show off," so we also allow individual run-throughs for those who wish.

We give everyone a graduation certificate, then end the evening with a spay-neuter pep talk, answer questions, and give out the final homework assignment. We also tell them to "pick up the phone and give us a call if any questions arise in the future." But they usually don't want to leave and ask if there's another class. SuperPuppy Class has advanced levels, so we explain them and demonstrate with our dogs before saying good-bye. If it's been a good SuperPuppy Class, over 80% of the people who started will graduate!

Best Instructors for SuperPuppy Class

As you can see, SuperPuppy Class is quite different than either a K.P.T. socialization experience or Basic Obedience. But, in order for SuperPuppy Class to work, it needs the *best* teachers and trainers your clinic, club or organization has. Notice, I said teachers, as well as trainers. SuperPuppy Class needs instructors who are able to teach people as well as dogs!

In many training programs, new instructors start out teaching in Beginners classes because these classes are less complicated and demanding than Advanced. Little or no attention is given to anyone's ability to teach people. This won't work in SuperPuppy Class for three big reasons:

1. SuperPuppy Class focuses upon helping new pet owners overcome at-home behavior problems. Given different life-styles and the wide variety of problems puppies pose, only very experienced instructors will be able to sort everything out and offer advice that works.

2. Because SuperPuppy Class starts with impressionable puppies, instructors have to be able to call upon all their knowledge and experience to make sure NONE of the puppies are worse off for coming to class.

3. Finally, the instructors have to do all this in a way NUPOs can understand, and without offending them. If you don't allow NUPOs to feel good about themselves while they're learning new complicated things, they'll just drop out.

SuperPuppy Class is a real challenge for everyone involved, and total involvement, with the *best* possible people, is what you need to have a successful puppy class!

*Conformation people can practice stacking instead of the Sit/Wait.

ORIENTATION

Beginning SuperPuppy Class meets once weekly for seven sessions. The first meeting is an Orientation meeting without the dogs. The entire family is encouraged to attend. The chief purpose of the Orientation is to begin the difficult process of re-education without the distracting influence of the puppies. I try to keep the Orientation humorous and informative. Slides, videos, and live demos are used to illustrate the topics covered. The Orientation lasts about ninety minutes. Even with all the teaching aids, anything longer leads to loss of attention.

First, I congratulate everyone on caring enough to come to class. I then talk about the disastrous pet owner failure rate and state the class goal — not just to help them raise a pretty good dog, but to raise a great pet, *the best dog they'll ever have!*

Next we discuss and show some of the many things dogs do for us: make people laugh and smile, find lost kids, help us recover from illness, injury and loss of loved ones, help to put dinner on the table, remove people from harm, warn of possible danger, work in the military, watch our property and belongings, help some of us see and hear and become independent, find illegal drugs and explosives, apprehend criminals, manage and protect livestock.

Wolves and Dogs

Next, I talk about the pack life of the wolf. Since the family dog is almost certainly descended from wild canines, understanding of how these animals live and raise their young can be extremely helpful in puppy rearing and training.

I explain that wild canine research shows clearly that modern selective breeding hasn't created the dog, just emphasized or de-emphasized specific traits present in wolves and other canines. A good example would be herding. Watching Border Collies work livestock is very similar to watching wolves stalk and kill caribou. The big difference is most Border Collies are no longer *that* interested in making mutton stew.

Then, slides and videos of domestic dogs raising their puppies are shown. The topics of learning and memory, subordination, communication, and early stimulation spring from these images. By comparing the behaviors and body signals of dogs and wolves, NUPOs can see for themselves just how similar to wolves their puppies really are.

Re-Education

The comparison between wolves and dogs is an important part of re-education because, before they can communicate effectively with their puppies, NUPOs need an accurate, sensible explanation of what the dog is, and why he does what he does.

Hardly anyone comes to Orientation with the notion that their pup is more of a wolf than any other living mammal. More often than not, they have some kind of idea that Waldo is more like a kid with a fur coat — a hyperactive, brain-damaged, retarded, slightly deaf, unintelligible, vindictive child, but a fur-coated kid no less!

In order for them to teach successfully, they'll have to learn to view their puppy as a highly-evolved, intelligent member of another species — not a defective member of the human race!

A Den-Dwelling Animal

Canines are one of the most social of all species. They raise and care for their young well past the juvenile stage of development. Many other mammals, such as the felines, tend to their young only until they're juveniles, and then the juveniles must fend for themselves. Most feline mothers raise their kits alone, while wolves and many other canines raise their cubs in families. Adult males, as well as females, take part in cub rearing!

A few NUPOs know this, but what they're not aware of is how it translates into puppy rearing practices. One slide shows wolf cubs howling and crying. I ask "Does anyone know why they're doing this?" Someone usually volunteers, "Because they're hungry?" I then show a slide of a puppy crying and howling while barricaded in the kitchen along with a full food bowl.

Next I tell them that very young canines will almost always cry when separated from their mother. This appears to be a reaction typical of the species, most likely genetically based. Why should this behavior be so persistent? Most often, the reason for species-wide behavior lies in survival. If very young cubs were separated from their mother, they just wouldn't make it through the night as they're too dependent upon her for food, shelter, warmth, and protection.

Researchers have recorded the distress cries of young canines and played them back in the presence of adults. The older animals immediately try to locate the phantom puppies! This is another clue that indicates separation stress reactions have survival value because they help insure that a separated, distressed infant will be rescued.

Fear of Being Alone

Cubs seem to be born with a "fear of being alone." When their physiological reactions are measured while they're howling, whining, and crying, researchers found these reactions correlate with fear responses.

When the cubs are around four to five weeks of age, mother can leave them for brief periods. However, they are not left entirely alone. An adult pack member stays with them. Most of them show little sign of distress which indicates the stress reaction is being modified in intensity, probably due to aging.

This is important information as many NUPOs believe the puppy may be "angry" because it's left alone. If it causes damage or eliminates, "It's doing so out of spite!" Nothing could be further from the truth!

The Artificial Den

Next, I show wolf cubs nursing in their den. I explain that in nature this is where they're born and raised. I then show a slide of a Shetland Sheepdog mom nursing her puppies in a covered, den-like, whelping box. This helps them see that dens are natural shelters for canines.

Nancy and I strongly recommend that they begin to think about providing their puppies with an "artificial den." We tell them that den training is the only reliable way we know to keep the puppy calm when it's alone, and also to ensure it's safe and secure and doesn't get into mischief when unattended.

Nancy, as a breeder, informs them that every puppy she places MUST go to that new home with a den! People will not get a puppy from her unless they commit themselves to using the den, and her puppies are not placed until they are calm and quiet in the den overnight and when no one's around for several hours during the day.

We list all the ways they can use the den now and in the future. I tell them, "The den is not only a *must* for housetraining, but once the pup is den-trained, you'll be able to find many other uses for it. If your dog should injure himself or become ill, the den will be invaluable during recovery. If you move, his adjustment to your new home will be quicker and less stressful. If you travel by car and have the room, placing him in the den will protect him from abrupt changes in speed or direction. If you stay at motels, hotels, or at aunt Edna's, you can be sure that he'll be 'damage-proof' if his den is available. Lapses in housetraining, at any age, can easily be corrected with the den. Since it's portable, you'll always have a place to keep your pup comfortably when he cannot be watched — no matter where you are. And, he'll always have a special, safe place to go when he needs to 'get away from it all.'"

One of the objections NUPOs have about using crates is locking the dog into a small, confining space. To remind them that they, as mothers and fathers, at one time "den trained" their kids, we show slides of toddlers in their cribs and playpens. We even have pictures of our grandson, Jason, in our dog, Kis's, den and Kis in Jason's playpen!

I assure them that they needn't rush home and throw their pup into an old playpen, but we'd like them to start thinking about den-training. It should be done over a weekend using the procedure in their *SuperPuppy* books.

Den Training Objections

Once their fear of "dog jail" is alleviated, their big objection is that they now they have more work to do and have to spend more money! Also, some of them want the dog outside all the time, not in the house.

We explain that the relatively small amount of extra effort spent now will prevent all kinds of extra work and expense later on. The extra investment could save them big bucks because, if Waldo hasn't damaged the backyard or laundry room or garage or kitchen yet, give him a few more weeks or months! We then show pictures of damage done by non-den-trained dogs when left alone.

I sum up by saying, "Because the dog is highly social and intelligent, we can live with it like no other species, but if you want a super puppy, you have to be aware of *its* needs. When you're raising your puppy, don't leave it alone any more than necessary. Remember, in nature, canine cubs are *never* alone.

"By den-training, you can properly prepare your puppy for those times when it *has* to be alone. You can introduce the den and/or exercise pen over a weekend, using the method in your *SuperPuppy* books. If you're gone for more than four hours during the day, set up the den inside an exercise pen and remove the den door.

Make sure the pup isn't wearing a collar and has water and something safe to chew. *Never, ever* leave the puppy tied up alone, inside or out, and *never, ever* give the puppy the unsupervised run of the place, inside or out. Later on, after puberty, when it's grown-up and you have helped it become a confident, well-behaved adult, it'll be ready for that freedom!"

Socialization

Dog training classes train people to train dogs, but one very important class learning experience for puppies has to do with the new people and puppies they meet.

Researchers have found that very young pups *must* be regularly exposed to people to prevent a subsequent fear of people. We tell the NUPOs about this and mention that their homework will include having the puppy meet someone new *every* day. This means they should take the dog places, not just wait at home for someone to come over.

We suggest they start socializing their pups by having them meet relatives and neighbors. Once they go through this list, they can always find strangers out for a walk who would love to say "hello" to a cute little puppy. Other places to socialize are playgrounds or shopping malls. If their puppies are not too large, we advise the NUPOs to pick them up, so the greeting is done at eye level. We also caution them to hold their puppies by the collar when they meet new dogs. This helps bashful puppies be less intimidated and more open and allows the NUPO better control.

Early Stimulation

Research shows that when dogs are given lots of different, challenging things to do when growing up, they learn better when adults, and they are less fearful of new things! Natural caution won't be blunted, but unwarranted fears produced by novelty can be controlled. Inappropriate fear can cripple. It prevents the dog from reaching its potential or worse — it could lead to euthanasia.

Environmental stimulation is an important aspect of raising a super puppy. We show pictures of wolf cubs growing up surrounded by natural conditions. Their dens are usually located near running water and amidst a variety of flora and fauna. There's always something new to do — trying to discover where the beetle went when it disappeared behind the rock; wondering what is that thing that looks like a walking pincushion; and what happens when you fall off the log into the creek!

In trying to keep our puppies safe from disease and out of harm's way, we have taken away much of the beneficial stimulation from the young dog, thus removing a very important part of growing up. If we invent interesting things for them to do and challenges for them to overcome, we'll be putting back this needed stimulation.

I show slides of very young puppies playing on tiny puppy obstacles. Our favorite is a shot of a five-week-old sliding down a two-and-a-half foot incline into a Mr. Turtle wading pool containing several inches of water!

We tell NUPOs that their homework will include taking Waldo or Wanda to a new place AT LEAST three times a week. This can be done in conjunction with socialization. We tell them that the last three weeks of class will include challenging obstacles, and I show slides of previous classes using the obstacles.

Communication

When you ask NUPOs about canine communication, they'll usually mention sound first. People are so used to thinking in terms of using speech in communication, that they automatically think that the dog also relies predominantly upon sound. We have to remind them that, although dogs, wolves, and other canines use sounds, their primary channels of communication are posturing or body language, and scents.

If a wolf were to lose its vocal ability because of some illness or injury, it could still effectively communicate and maintain its position within the pack. It would have a very difficult time however, if it somehow "forgot" its body language or could no longer smell!

Although wolves use a variety of sounds in communication, these sounds seem to be concerned with emotional states like, "I'm hurt, hungry, horny, lost, lonely, angry, irritated, pleased, excited, or frightened."

Human speech, on the other hand, is a different phenomenon altogether. Babies start out using sounds to communicate basic emotional states, but between one and two years of age begin to form new sounds that are not necessarily involved with these states. Then they do something that the pup never does — children begin putting these sounds together into sentences!

The point we try to make is that the dog's chief way of communicating doesn't necessarily involve sound. Although they do use sounds and can learn to respond to many different sounds, unlike children, they do not acquire a grammar. As far as their use of sounds is concerned, they're eternal infants!

Slides are shown of the rich and varied postures dogs use in communication. We also discuss their preoccupation with scents and what they can tell about the world through smells.

Learning and Memory

Perhaps the most widely misunderstood area of puppy rearing concerns how dogs learn. Ninety-nine NUPOs out of one hundred will try to teach by talking and ignore body language. They are confused about the distinction between sounds and grammar. I tell them, "Although the dog can learn to respond to many different words and phrases, these words and phrases derive their influences or 'meanings' from their association with certain actions." We call these Teaching Actions.

One example I use is taken from the canine weaning process. I show slides of a Golden Retriever mom "talking" to her puppy. She has just pinned the youngster to the ground and is growling at him.

I tell them, "If she had growled at the pup before she pinned him, the puppy probably would have ignored her. It would have kept trying to nurse! It would *not* automatically respond to the sound of her growl. Later, all she'll need to do is look the pup in the eye and growl. That will stop it dead in its tracks! But, the pup has to learn the meaning of the growl through Mom's actions. Pinning the puppy to the ground was her Teaching Action."

Fast Feedback

In conjunction with Teaching Actions, we begin to stress the importance of Fast Feedback. Many NUPOs feel they can discipline a dog minutes or hours after the fact. I tell them that the question of delays in canine learning has been thoroughly studied and ask them how long they think feedback can be delayed and still permit the pup to learn. Sometimes someone will guess seconds, but usually I have to tell them that, under ideal lab conditions, most puppies could only learn if the delay between their actions and some cue signaling forthcoming reward or safety was under FIVE seconds!

I ask them, "Imagine you're teaching Waldo to do something like sit. How long would you wait before rewarding Waldo after he sat?" Almost everyone agrees they would not wait but reward him as soon as he sits. Then I ask, "How long do you suppose it would take to teach him to sit if you waited over an hour? Forever, right? How about five minutes? How about five seconds? Even if you wait five seconds, it may take forever!" Then I explain that the rules are the same for learning *to do* something and learning *not to do* something. The dog doesn't have two brains — one for learning what to do and another for learning what *not* to do!

Remembering Past Events

NUPOs do not seem to understand how canine memory works. Almost all of them think they can drag Waldo over to some mess he's made and get him to remember what he did minutes or hours before by saying something like, "Did you do this? Did *you* do this to my carpet!?" (Who did they think did it, the Poop Fairy?) "Baaaad dog! Baaad Waldo! Smack! "Now get outside and stay there!"

I try to sort out this memory business by using an example from the *SuperPuppy* booklet. "If Waldo smells food scraps in the wastebasket and then tips the basket over and eats, he'll remember this and may try it again. His action, knocking over the wastebasket, produces an immediate pleasant result, food. But if the action produces an unpleasant result — if the food is bitter, or the falling wastebasket frightens him — chances are that he won't bother the basket again.

"If you would take him over to the mess and 'talk tough' to him, he wouldn't be able to recall knocking over the basket. However, if the situation reoccurred, i.e., being alone in the kitchen just after you left for work with the basket smelling great, he would remember that knocking over the basket led to goodies!"

I sum up by saying, "Puppies learn quickly, provided you remember to use Teaching Actions and provided they receive Fast Feedback. This means that when you're in the laundry room, and the pup's in the family room, you have a potential problem. If he starts to eliminate on the floor and nothing happens that *instant*, he'll most likely do it again. As far as housetraining is concerned, there's nothing effective you can do when you get back to the family room, even if you 'rub his nose in it!' If you try this, he'll probably wind up learning not to eliminate only when you're around and to scram or cower if you show up when there's a mess on the floor."

Demonstrations

If we have a puppy at Orientation, there are various learning demonstrations that we can do. To show the differences between sounds, grammar, and body language, I can do one or more of the following: teach the pup to come over when I say, "Hawaii!," teach it to come when I whistle three times, and to sit when I whistle once, then teach it to do all of these activities using only hand signals.

Also, I can teach Sit using hand signals then, start saying, "Touch your toes." Drop out the hand signal, and presto! — he's sitting on, "Waldo, touch your toes." That usually gets a nice laugh. Or I could teach him *not* to pick up a treat when I say, "OK," and to pick it up when I say, "NO."

In order to demonstrate the effects of delays upon learning, I toss a treat with my right hand, count to five, and say, "Erhhh." If I do this in a conversational tone, most pups will ignore the sound, and pick up the treat. I do this three times.

Before I toss the fourth treat, I say, "Erhhh," again, but pop the leash. I then toss another treat and wait to see if the pup moves toward it. If he does, I say, "Erhhh," and pop the leash again. I then say, "All right," and offer a treat with my left hand.

Most pups will learn to stop going for the treat when they hear, "Erhhh," after two or three leash pops. The NUPOs can now see the effect of fast, immediate feedback!

Next I smack my lips and drop a treat using my left hand. The pup takes it. I do this three times. Next, I drop the treat, but don't say anything. When the pup takes it, I count to five, then say, "Erhhh," in a conversational tone. I repeat and the NUPOs can see that waiting five seconds before saying, "Erhhh," neutralizes the voice correction, as it has no effect upon the pup taking the treat!

What I'm trying to get NUPOs to realize is the importance of Fast Feedback in learning and that the puppy will never learn the grammatical or deep meaning of sentences. What they learn is the tone or sound of the spoken words. This meaning is acquired through the pairing of sounds with Teaching Actions. We tell NUPOs that one of the things they'll be learning in class is which Teaching Actions to use in particular situations.

I sum up by saying, "You teach puppies by *doing* something, not by *talking*. Words are only for human convenience, because once the dog has learned something, you can then use the associated words to cue the learned behavior. But remember, with the right Teaching Actions, dogs can learn just as well using whistles or hand signals. If you were to become unable to speak because of an accident or illness, you could still raise and train a dog to do just about anything it's able to do!"

Subordination

The last set of slides shows both wolves and dogs performing subordination. After showing an older wolf pinning several youngsters, I show a Sheltie mom pinning her puppies. Their body postures are almost identical! Raven, the Sheltie, is subordinating her pup at weaning time. I explain to the NUPOs that, "This is a normal part of growing up. In the wild *all* able adults pin down or subordinate the cubs before they're twenty weeks old. The dam, however, begins the process at weaning. After Raven subordinated her puppies, they didn't *fear* her. They still played with her and nursed occasionally. The important thing is that she could stop them any time she *chose to*. All she needed to do was stand tall, growl, and look them in the eye.

"The closest human label that I can think of for this is 'respect.' The pups were already bonded to her so there was mutual affection between them. What was missing was respect. Up until weaning, the youngsters could do pretty much what they wanted. They jumped up and climbed all over her, pulled her ears and tail, nipped her muzzle, and ate whenever they wanted to –– sort of like what Waldo is doing now, right? After subordination they bowed down and licked her muzzle whenever she gave them the 'eye'."

Submission vs. Fear

The chief NUPO objection to subordination concerns "breaking the dog's spirit." Many NUPOs want their dogs to protect their property and back them up if they're accosted, so they're looking for a high-spirited companion, not a wimp. They don't want the dog to cower and urinate every time they come in the door!

I explain to them that subordination and fear are two different things. Researchers have measured the physiological responses of dogs signaling subordinance and found them to be quite different from fear reactions. Breathing and heart rate *decrease* during the normal subordinate greeting, not increase as would be expected if fear were present!

We have slides of the different body postures associated with fear and the subordinate greeting. I explain that in the canine social greeting, the low ranking animal greets with its tail down and wagging vigorously. The ears are back, the lips are drawn up into a "grin," and it may lick the higher ranking animal's muzzle.

Fear, on the other hand, is characterized by trying to *stay away* from whomever or whatever causes it. The tail is tucked tightly underneath the body, the ears are back, the body is trembling, and, if cornered, the animal may defecate, urinate, or bite.

Sometimes, excitable young pups are overly submissive when they greet and may urinate while crouching or jumping up. If a NUPO's puppy does this, I explain that the last thing they should do is punish the dog for breaking housetraining because this will make the problem worse and could lead to fear. At this age, when they're excited, many puppies haven't gained reliable control over their urinary sphincter — they urinate involuntarily. If they are not disciplined, most puppies will stop urinating submissively by the time they pass through puberty. If a NUPO's dog urinates during the greeting, I tell them, "Until Wanda gets a little older, don't make a big deal about saying 'hello.' Excitement will lead to loss of control. Try saying 'hello' with a toy, treat, or other item that will distract from the social aspects of the greeting.

Friendship and Respect

"If you want your dogs to grow up to be your close friends, and respectful, well-behaved members of your families, you *must* make sure you can look them in the eye, stand up straight, and raise your voice so they stop whatever they're doing, report back to you with tail wagging, wearing a 'grin,' ready to lick your hands or faces. Once they come to view you as if you were their real moms or dads, they won't try to challenge your authority, but will work with you on those things you feel are important.

"As far as protection is concerned, almost all older dogs will alert if there's a disturbance in their 'territory.' Your job will be to check out the disturbance, then get them quiet, as 99.99% of the time it will be a false alarm. For the family dog, alerting is a valuable job, and a good alerting bark will often discourage intruders.

"Since the chief nonmedical reason dogs are put to sleep is because they bite someone they shouldn't, your ability to control their natural territorial and protective tendencies is essential. Remember, a law enforcement dog stops *whatever* it's doing when it's handler commands 'out' or 'aus.' Mutual respect is an all-important aspect of the man/dog relationship."

Concluding the Orientation

Before saying good night we talk about chewing and how to manage it. Most of the chewing recommendations are in their *SuperPuppy* books, so I briefly review these chapters and refer them to the written material if they have questions.

Finally, we discuss their first homework assignment. If they haven't already done so, NUPOs are asked to get their pups used to the collar and leash. A handout describing the technique is provided. SuperPuppy Class uses "seat belt" buckle collars and six foot nylon leads. The *SuperPuppy* book tells them how to chew proof the leash. If someone asks why we don't use choke collars, I explain that once they're taught how to use the leash as a teaching tool, they won't need choke collars. Occasionally we do have to use a slip collar on a puppy, but it's a flat, nylon collar rather than a chain.

In order to prepare for First Puppy Night, they're asked to take the dog in the car to a new location *every* day. Once they arrive at the new location, they should let the puppy pull them around on the leash and meet as many new people as possible. We caution them not to pull or jerk on the leash, and NEVER drag or force their pup in any way! If the dog is hesitant about meeting people, we suggest they pick it up, or if it's a large puppy, hold it by the collar, so it cannot avoid the greeting.

The homework will help accustom the dog to car rides so it doesn't arrive at First Puppy Night carsick and disoriented. We want the pups pulling the NUPOs with lots of vim and vigor when they come to class. They should be used to car rides, going to strange locations, and meeting new people well before First Puppy Night!

We also suggest not feeding the puppy after twelve noon on each class date. Water should always be available. The reason for this is to help Waldo and Wanda ride easier in the car as the ride to class may be fairly long. Also we've found the pups are more alert and eager to learn at class if they don't have full stomachs!

All that remains is to enroll the NUPOs. When everyone first arrived at Orientation, they received an enrollment form, a *SuperPuppy* book, reminder list of things to bring First Puppy Night, and their homework. The reminder list includes:

1. Inoculation records. When the NUPOs first contacted us about class, we asked them to bring the records to Orientation if possible. We also volunteer to call the veterinarian to verify records. We've learned the hard way that the time to check shot records is not First Puppy Night!

2. Unbreakable water dish.

3. Leash and collar.
4. Loose, comfortable clothing and rubber-soled shoes.
5. Training treats.
6. Waldo or Wanda.

*Copies of this handout and other class handouts are reproduced at the end of the manual.

" WANDA "

FIRST PUPPY NIGHT

Since some of the puppies are apprehensive when they arrive at class, our first job is to determine to what degree. When a puppy walks in, tail up and barking, we immediately show the NUPO how to quiet it using a leash correction along with a raised voice, followed by praise and a food reward. If a puppy is hesitant about walking, we immediately have the NUPO pick it up and carry it or stop and wait for it to initiate movement. Usually, these are the two extremes that indicate stress. If we can get the owners to deal with the pups' apprehensions right away, we can prevent them from getting worse.

The next thing I do is greet every pup at eye level with a treat. The main reason I use food is to continue to determine the stress level. I ask the NUPOs to pick up the smaller pups, and I crouch down to greet the larger ones. If they eat the treat, they're usually telling me, "Not too upset." If they avoid me or act threatening, I ask the NUPO to hold them firmly by the collar, and I try again. If the puppy still refuses, I mark this on the chart and try again later.

I don't feel it's necessarily an act of misbehavior if a class puppy doesn't care to greet a stranger or allow a stranger to touch it. It could indicate a timid pup who's responding because of limited or incomplete socialization, a pup who's been mistreated by people in the past, or one who's reacting to the stress of being in a new, unfamiliar environment with lots of strange dogs and people.

If the pup just received an inoculation, it may not wish to be touched because of some tenderness or discomfort. Puppies who come in with their ears in racks may not want to be touched by strangers. In other words, there are a host of reasons for not participating in the greeting, and it's better to wait and get more information about what may be going on than to correct the dog inappropriately and prematurely.

Collar Check

I then make sure the collar fits properly. We encourage the use of "seat belt" or Snap-Lock® collars because they're very easy to put on and take off, and can be adjusted so they fit precisely. They are called seat belt collars because they snap together and adjust like an automobile seat belt. Regular buckle collars are also appropriate for SuperPuppy Class. If I can get one finger easily between the collar and the pup's neck, the pup won't be able to slip out and will still be comfortable.

Shot Records

After I greet the NUPOs, as well as the puppies, I ask them to check in with Nancy. She makes sure the inoculation records are in order. All shots must be up-to-date. We require DHLPP,

Corona, and Bordetella. If there's a problem, we ask the NUPO please to put the puppy in the car until we can sort it out. We are very careful that NO PUPPY stays at class unless properly inoculated. We have already explained the need for proper inoculations and records at Orientation. We do not allow ANYONE into class *unless they've attended Orientation* and can show proof of inoculations. We even offer to call their veterinarian before First Puppy Night to confirm inoculations. Due to all the preparation, we usually don't have a problem with shot records.

Benefits Justify Risks

Because SuperPuppy Class starts with dogs under sixteen weeks, it's essential that EVERY precaution be taken to guard against the transmission of viral and bacterial diseases. Even with all the safeguards, there will always be a small risk. We feel the benefits of starting at this age far outweigh this risk. It makes no sense to me to have a six-month-old physically healthy dog who's heading for the animal shelter because it never learned to control its impulses; nor does it make sense to keep show dogs sheltered from the world when they're growing up — what you often wind up with is a great looking "nut case!"

Movement Helps Adjustment

While we're waiting to get started, we have the NUPOs walk their pups around the training area, but ask them *not* to socialize with the other NUPOs and their pups. The reason for this is to get the dogs more comfortable with their surroundings and to guard against any possible social threat or unpleasantness. We ask the NUPOs to offer a treat periodically and to let us know if the pup refuses to take it. Again, we're trying to identify those puppies who seem to be having difficulty adjusting.

If we find a pup who will not move or eat, and it's too large for the NUPO to pick up and carry, we ask the owner to have a seat and hold the dog between their legs. The dog is also sitting and facing forward. In order to prevent the puppy from hiding out, the NUPO holds the pup with one hand on the collar and the other across the chest. Some puppies need more time to collect themselves. If no pressure is put upon them to do anything, they seem to adapt more quickly. But, we don't think it's beneficial for them to hide out behind Mom's or Dad's feet or underneath the bench. The idea is to show these pups that nothing bad is going to happen to them, so they might as well stick around to find out if something good turns up!

The Listening Position

Class officially begins with the NUPOs seated on benches. We ask them to put their puppies in the Listening Position. Nancy demonstrates the Listening Position. We've found it more effective if she does the demonstrations. A woman NUPO may feel that the only reason Waldo starts to "listen" is because he's responding to a man's authority, so she misses the other nuances involved in teaching the pup to settle.

Next, Nancy "asks" the puppy if it wants to come with her. If it says, "No," she uses another pup. She explains to the NUPOs that if she doesn't pick their puppy to use to demonstrate, it's not because that dog isn't smart enough; it's because she's not going to force a puppy to come with her against its will.

Depending upon size, the pup is either put on the NUPO's lap or seated between the NUPO's legs. We ask the NUPOs to grasp the pup's neck scruff with the strong hand, after hooking a thumb underneath the collar. The other hand is placed across the pup's chest. If at any time a dog should become disruptive by bothering its neighbor, barking, whining, or squirming, we ask its NUPO to raise his or her voice and shake the pup by the scruff. When the puppy settles, the NUPO should praise and stroke it. We ask the NUPOs to interrupt us at any time to do this.

LARGER PUP: Note how hand grasps neck scruff as well as collar.

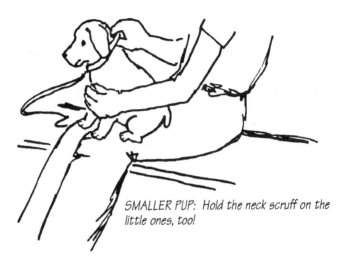

SMALLER PUP: Hold the neck scruff on the little ones, too!

Don't Say "No"

We also ask them *not* to say, "No," when they raise their voices. We tell them that unless "No" causes the pup to stop whatever it's doing and report in, it's best to start fresh with a new sound. Since they say "No" to the kids, the pup should have its *own* "No" sound.

We suggest using "Erhhh," a half bark, half growl sound similar to the canine mother's weaning reprimand. I remind them that the dog is learning the meaning of this sound through association with the scruff shake Teaching Action. The main reason for changing to a non-English Stop Signal is to begin the difficult task of teaching NUPOs *not* to teach their pups by talking. Starting class with a different Stop Sound helps them begin to learn this and causes the puppy less confusion.

Disruptive Puppy

Sometimes there's a pup who won't settle for it's owner. If we have a dog who's still disruptive after three scruff shakes, we ask the NUPO if it's OK to use the pup for a demonstration. Usually, a disruptive puppy will want to get up and go with Nancy! She demonstrates the Listening Position, and if she cannot get the pup to settle after three attempts, we ask the NUPO to take the dog for a short walk, but keep within earshot.

The reason Nancy doesn't press the issue is because, if she can't get the puppy to settle after three attempts, it's usually because the pup isn't mature enough to hold still for any period of time.

After a week or two the NUPO will be able to hold it in the Listening Position, but until then, we have him or her walk the pup around when it becomes restless.

If the pup is still disruptive while walking, I take the NUPO off to the side while Nancy continues the class. *We don't ignore any puppy showing signs of apprehension or distress.* If you do, the pup usually doesn't calm down, continues to have a bad time, and the class has a hard time concentrating on anything but the upset dog.

Threatening Behavior

When everyone is reasonably settled, we explain the ground rules. The instant any pup threatens anyone at class we expect that pup's owner to correct the threat. We consider threats to include barking, growling, nipping, and/or lip curling. If the pup is in the Listening Position, the Teaching Action is a scruff shake, accompanied by a firm "Erhhh." If the NUPOs are up on their feet, the appropriate Teaching Action is a leash pop, accompanied by "Erhhh." These corrections are followed by praise if the puppy settles.

We remind them that the number one nonmedical reason dogs are euthanatized is because they have bitten someone they shouldn't have. Unless someone at class is wearing a ski mask and carrying a lead pipe, the NUPOs need to correct threats *immediately*. We also tell them that if they cannot correct threatening behavior now, the chances of their being able to do so *after* the pup enters puberty are not very good.

NUPOs are often confused about this. Many feel that if they start disciplining the puppy for acting protectively, it will not be a good guard dog when it grows up. I explain that when they correct the threatening behavior directed toward individuals meaning them no harm, the pup learns to stop on the owner's command, something good, well trained, professional law enforcement dogs *must* all do. They are not teaching the pup never to threaten again, only that this isn't the appropriate time and not to do it anymore *right now!*

How to Greet

Another rule we have is for the NUPO to *ask* first before allowing his or her pup to greet another pup. The greeting should be controlled by both NUPOs holding the dogs by their collars and neck scruffs. The reason for this is to prevent any puppy, especially the small ones, from being overwhelmed by more exuberant, larger pups. Also, NUPOs will almost always get their leashes entangled if they allow their pups to interact freely. In the coming weeks, after they are more experienced and everyone is familiar with each other, this rule is relaxed.

Controlled Walking

The next topic is, "How to use the leash as a teaching tool instead of a tether." We use the Controlled Walking exercise to demonstrate proper use of the six-foot training leash. The goals are for NUPOs to teach the pups to walk without pulling and to keep up with changes in direction and pace without being underfoot. The pups are not required to Heel or to walk on the left side during the introduction.

Nancy tries to pick a puppy that is naturally a great puller. Before she begins, she lets the dog pull her all over the place. We caution everyone *not* to teach Controlled Walking unless their dogs *first* pull them around because it's very easy to cause a lagging problem if a puppy is corrected when it's *not* pulling forward. We feel the first step in teaching Controlled Walking is to teach *forward pulling*. If we have conformation pups, we split them into a Gaiting Group where they concentrate on forward pulling!

There may be several pups who are hesitant about moving. We form a Bashful Group and work with it separately from the Pullers. In this group the NUPOs are asked to walk several feet away, crouch down, and praise profusely. When the pup comes over, it's given a food reward. This is done three times in a row, and then they take a break before trying again. For a more detailed explanation of this method, see "Introducing the Leash" and "Alternative Procedure" in the Handouts section of this manual.

During the break, we have them sit in a circle and hold the pup between their legs in the Listening Position. After several minutes the bashful pups usually begin to "say hello" to each other! The NUPOs allow them to greet, and this seems to break the ice. They start moving around within the circle, interacting cautiously. After about five minutes, we do more leash work using the Crouch and Praise Method.

Teaching Controlled Walking

After Nancy demonstrates the procedure, we teach Controlled Walking to the NUPOs in the following way:

1. The leash is held with both hands in the leash loop, palms down, waist high, and slightly out from the body. The knuckles should *always* be kept pointing directly at the puppy.

2. The NUPOs start by giving the verbal signal, "Waldo, let's go for a walk!" in a firm, happy tone of voice, followed immediately by high-energy praise, Happy Talk, that is continued throughout the Teaching Segment.

3. If the puppy starts to pull, the NUPO is instructed to pop the leash right before it becomes taut, providing a Teaching Action that indicates to the pup that it has made a wrong choice. *No* verbal corrections are used.

4. To signal the end of the lesson the NUPO makes a smacking, kissing sound with the lips (the "smack-smack" sound), drops down and offers the pup a treat, and pets for several seconds. The reason we have them drop down on the "smack-smack" sound is to begin setting up the Recall exercise that will be introduced next class meeting.

5. NUPOs must then *allow* the dog to pull for a minute or so. This is called the Time Out, and concludes a Teaching Segment.

6. During some of the Time Outs we ask the NUPOs to have their puppies meet each other. We start with pups about the same size greeting one-on-one. The pups are held by the collar and neck scruff, while the owners introduce themselves and say hello.

The problems NUPOs seem to have learning the Controlled Walking procedure are:

1. They are not exuberant enough with their praise or forget it entirely.

2. They keep stopping to straighten the leash.

3. The leash pop is ineffective because of poor timing, incorrect intensity, or both.

4. The training walk is too long.

5. They forget to hold the leash correctly and to point their knuckles at the pup.

Tail Wagging Contest

In order to help overcome these difficulties we do the following:

1. Before anyone starts teaching Controlled Walking, we rehearse praising by having a Tail Wagging Contest. Everyone holding a leash is asked to bring his or her pup out and stand about six feet apart. The others are asked to judge. Using verbal praise, the NUPOs must get their pups' tails wagging without moving around or touching them. When we say, "Go," they begin praising, and when we say, "Time Out," they make the "smack-smack" sound, drop down, and give the pups a treat. Having a Tail Wagging Contest helps many NUPOs overcome inhibitions as everyone is suddenly making crazy fools of themselves. And the dogs love it! The judges usually pick three to four dogs, so we have a "wag off." The winning pup receives a rawhide chew and the winning NUPO receives a piece of jerky!

Helping the NUPO learn how to hold the leash.

2. To help them learn a proper leash pop, we have each NUPO individually show us how they're going to hold the leash. We ask them to give us a pop as we grasp the leash, and we offer suggestions based upon their performances.

3. To help them keep the leash from tangling and to make sure their corrections are effective, we continually remind them to keep their KNUCKLES POINTED AT THE PUP'S HEAD, even if this means walking sideways, backward, or spinning around! If they try to transfer the leash behind their backs, they can't correct if the pup pulls, and, if they choke up on the leash, the leash pop becomes ineffective.

4. To make sure no one overdoes the training walk, we start with a five second Teaching Segment and ask them to build up the time gradually so that, by next class meeting, they can teach for *one* minute before giving a Time Out. At home the Time Out should be at least three minutes, and we remind them that during the Time Out the pups are allowed to pull and/or play.

5. After everyone has a chance to practice, we ask them to take a seat, and Nancy re-demonstrates the procedure. Their homework handout has everything in writing, so they can refresh their memories before working.

Double Learning

Teaching people motor skills is nothing like teaching concepts! They may understand intellectually what we're trying to demonstrate, but not be able to get their bodies to go along with the program. We have to be very patient with NUPOs who don't seem to be able to put it all together. Some might be taking medication that could affect timing and movement. Others may have disabilities such as weak backs or arthritis. Still others are not naturally well-coordinated. If someone is having trouble executing, it's best to have a private talk with that person and offer extra after class help.

We all know that learning new physical skills requires repeated rehearsal before the part of our brains responsible for motor movement is properly programmed. This means that NUPOs will need to practice repeatedly before they even begin to become smooth and coordinated. To help prevent the pup from paying the price during this period, the Teaching Segments are kept very short with relatively longer Time Outs.

Feedback and Consistency

I sum up Controlled Walking by saying, "The reason Nancy is quickly able to teach the pup not to pull when she says, 'Waldo, let's go for a walk,' is because the *instant* before Waldo tries to pull, the leash makes him uncomfortable. He can figure out how to prevent this from happening because of Fast Feedback and consistency. Nancy uses Happy Talk or verbal praise to let Waldo know she's not angry with him and to keep reminding him where she is because, if he stays near her, nothing unpleasant will happen to him.

"In other words, what Nancy's doing is arranging the world in such a way that Waldo can make up his own mind how to behave. He's given choices. He can freely choose what to do. He's not forced to do Nancy's bidding. If he chooses to not pull and stay near Nancy, nothing unpleasant happens to him. If he chooses to continue to try to pull, the leash makes life uncomfortable. Nancy's job is to make him an offer he can't refuse!"

After answering questions, we take a five to ten minute water break.

Assigning Groups

For the second half of First Puppy Night we divide the class into Teaching Groups. Puppies are assigned to groups based upon temperament, age, and size. Groups are no larger than eight dogs. The reasons for having Teaching Groups are:

1. People seem to learn better if they feel more at ease and part of the class and receive individual attention.
2. The instructors can become more involved in class as each instructor is responsible for his or her Group. They have to learn the names of the people and dogs in their Group and use their names when teaching. If a NUPO has questions during the week, he or she can contact their Group Leader.

3. If someone misses class and doesn't contact anyone, it's the Group Leader's responsibility to find out what happened. If the NUPO can't make a class, the Group Leader can mail the homework.

4. Pups of similar temperaments and ages seem to relate better, and their owners have more in common.

Two Part Discussion

In Group, we first discuss at-home problems. The discussion is divided into two parts. Tonight we focus upon those problems that occur when the NUPO is home and able to work with the pup. Next week we'll talk about the problems that arise when the NUPO isn't home, or the pup is unsupervised. We also wait until next class before we teach them how to correct Waldo when he jumps up, nips, mouths, or barks at them *personally*. We tell them that the reason for this is that they need to go through one week of subordination before they'll have the necessary power and authority to correct pushy behavior directed toward them.

The very first thing we do in Group is introduce everyone. Then we ask them to tell us about their at-home concerns. Usually they mention jumping up, mouthing, housetraining, rough play, digging, begging during mealtime, food stealing, destructive chewing, barking, growling, and not listening.

Exercise is Crucial

Before going any further, we make them aware that all of the training in the world isn't going to help one iota if Waldo isn't getting enough running. We tell them that a young, healthy dog needs to run *flat out* until it tires, at least *twice* per day — once in the morning and once in the evening. This is a basic need. Just as food, water, shelter, and companionship are vital for survival, regular running is essential for mental health — theirs as well as the pups'!

SuperPuppy and *How to Play With Your Dog!* have sections on exercise, and we ask if they have any questions. Usually, someone says that they take the dog for a daily run, but he still acts "hyper." We ask what they mean by run. If the pup is taken out for a jog or walk, and he's a young tiger like Waldo, this outing will hardly cause him to breathe hard.

In young canines, exercise means flat-out running, *not* jogging, trotting, or walking. We have to remind them that flat-out running is something young dogs do when they play with each other, and, when given the opportunity, playing with each other is something they do constantly! It's also important at this age for the young puppy to be able to set its own exercise pace and stop when tired.

We tell them the best way we know to provide daily exercise is to teach the pup to retrieve. Their *SuperPuppy* books have the "Best play retrieving method ever invented." Once learned, depending upon their pup's age, size, and breed, it will only take between five and fifteen minutes, twice a day, to provide adequate exercise.

Once the pup has been adequately exercised, the NUPO can concentrate upon correcting at-home behavior problems. Tonight we'll focus upon everything except what the dog does to them *personally*. Next week we'll show them what to do when Waldo jumps up, mouths, growls, or barks at them. Tonight we'll show them what to do when Waldo behaves this way toward others.

Teaching the Stop Signal

First, I pick out a puppy that is bouncing up during the greeting. I tell everyone to make believe this is my dog and ask for volunteer "visitors." I then have the "visitor" say hello to Waldo. As soon as he jumps, I toss a beanbag firmly at his rump and say, "Erhhh," *as it lands.* I *immediately* drop down, praise, pet, and give a treat. The "visitor" also drops down, praises, pets, and rewards. If my intensity and timing are good, it usually takes no more than two or three beanbag Teaching Actions, and Waldo is stopping on "Erhhh" alone. *Every* time he stops, he's rewarded.

Then we have everyone in Group try to get Waldo to jump up. They can do anything to entice him except actually calling him. Whenever he chooses not to jump, he's rewarded. If he forgets and starts to jump, he'll stop when he hears "Erhhh." If for some reason he ignores the Stop Sound, I toss the bag again and repeat the sound.

After we can't get him to jump up anymore, I explain, "The key to teaching Waldo good manners is to teach him the meaning of the Stop Sound. It usually takes *two* weeks to teach pups to stop reliably on signal. During these two weeks you should have a beanbag in one pocket, and treats in another, *whenever* you're with your pup.

We provide each NUPO with a beanbag at First Puppy Night. The beanbag is only a teaching aid. It's a *temporary* device used to provide fast, effective feedback, and, because it's associated with a unique sound, it helps give the Stop Sound its special meaning.

Use Set-Ups

During the next two weeks, the NUPOs are advised to create *all* those situations that have caused difficulty when they have been home with the dogs instead of waiting for them to occur naturally. I tell them that if they use setups, the dog will learn faster because he'll be getting more lessons, and they'll be prepared to teach every time the objectionable behavior occurs.

Restrictions on Tossing

I warn them to keep the beanbag out of sight at all times, and *only* use it if Waldo ignores the first "Erhhh." I also caution them *not* to throw anything at the pup when it does something objectionable directed at *them.*

Next week we'll demonstrate different Teaching Actions used for those situations. Finally, I caution them not to tell friends and neighbors who may be having problems with their dogs about the beanbag because, if used in the wrong circumstances and not properly executed, it could make a bad situation worse.

They can use the "Erhhh" Stop Sound, plus the beanbag if needed, to teach Waldo *all* of the manners they would like him to learn, provided they are prepared. This is why we divide the discussion of at-home behavior into several parts. Remember, on First Puppy Night we only discuss the objectionable things that Waldo does when the NUPO is home and able to intervene. Next week we talk about control during their absences.

The "Magic" Shaker Can

A "magic" device used in teaching dogs to stop barking on command is the shaker can. It's easily made from an aluminum beverage can and ten pennies. Initially, it's used like the beanbag, but it makes a sound that almost all dogs with normal hearing find unsettling. Since most dogs find the sound of the can unpleasant, we caution NUPOs to use it ONLY for barking and booby trapping.

Also, we have to make sure they understand why the dog is barking before they attempt to correct it. If Waldo is barking because he's out in the back yard alone and wants to be with someone, the last thing we want them to do is throw a can at him!

Territorial Barking

The can is primarily used to teach the dog to stop territorial barking on signal. Territorial barking is barking that occurs when there is some disturbance or perceived intrusion around the NUPO's property. I tell them, "Young dogs aren't very good at separating the good guys from the bad guys. If someone unfamiliar should approach the house or yard, they might bark. If they're not doing this now, they'll almost always start around puberty. If you don't have a way of getting them to hush when they bark at the wrong person, over time the barking will become more intense and indiscriminate and could eventually lead to biting.

Shaker Can Teaching Action

"When someone rings our doorbell and I have a young, untrained dog in the house, the first thing I do is get the can and put it behind my back. Next, I look out the window to see who it

is, and if they're not carrying machine guns and stilettos, I work with the pup *before* I open the door. I say, 'Erhhh,' and then put one finger to my mouth (Hush signal). Usually the dog will ignore this and continue barking. I then toss the can at the dog's feet and raise my voice just as it lands. Then, it's extremely important to *drop down and comfort the pup*, as the can will startle him if it's tossed properly. I use praise, petting, and treats when comforting. I then pick up the can and put it *behind* my back just in case the dog begins barking again.

"If my timing was good and my toss was hard enough, all I need to do, if the dog barks again, is to shake the can *behind* my back and say, 'Erhhh,' while giving the Hush hand signal. In fact I may not have to toss the can *ever* again! If needed, the sound it makes when I shake it behind my back will enforce the Stop signals.

"The reason for keeping the can out of sight is to prevent a dependency upon it. The goal is to teach the dog to quiet on signal. The signal is a verbal command and hand sign, *not* the sound of the can! The can is only a temporary training aid so should be as unnoticeable as possible before it's used."

What is Learned

Someone usually asks if the dog learns not to bark whenever the doorbell is rung. The answer is that almost all dogs will continue to bark when they first hear the doorbell, because the time delay between the onset of barking and the Teaching Action is too long. The goal is to have the dog stop barking whenever the Stop Signal is given, not to teach the dog to ignore the door bell or other cues indicating a territorial intrusion. I remind them that *all* well trained law enforcement dogs stop on command. If they don't, they shouldn't be used!

The reason we use a shaker can for territorial barking is that most aroused dogs are very intense and focused. We've found that many will not respond to a raised voice alone, or even a raised voice plus beanbag. But if someone has a noisy yet sensitive pup, be sure you recommend starting with the less startling Teaching Actions.

Take-Down for Subordination

The last thing that we cover is subordination. We save it for the end of the session because most of the pups are much easier to handle at that time. I demonstrate how to place the pup gently on its side without causing any discomfort.

The first step is to place the dog in the Listening Position while kneeling behind it. Because I'm right-handed, I roll him backward over my right leg until he's lying across it and then slide him down my leg. He winds up on his side with all four legs facing *away* from me. My right hand is still on the neck scruff, and my left hand rests on his midsection.

The key to this take-down method is to make sure the dog's rump remains on the ground when he's rolled back over the knee.

Restrain for Ten Seconds

Once Waldo is flat on the ground, he's not allowed to get up for ten seconds. If a pup should try to get up, its NUPO is instructed to raise his or her voice, "Erhhh," and shake the neck scruff.

After about ten seconds, all the NUPOs release the pups — IF THEY'RE QUIET — by making the "smack-smack" sound, picking up the leash, and standing up. They then praise, pet, and offer a food reward. They are cautioned *never* to let a pup up while it's struggling. If everything went well, they do two more Take Downs and gradually increase the down times.

We ask NUPOs not to talk to the pups when they first do the Take-Down because we've found that they can concentrate better on overcoming any attempt by the pups to get up. Also, if they begin praising before the pup has actually settled, the praise could initiate more struggling. After they're *sure* Waldo will no longer attempt to free himself before he's allowed to, they can praise and pet him while he's on his side.

Most Important Lesson

Of all the things we teach NUPOs at First Puppy Night, I feel subordination is the most important lesson. Unless a NUPO is able to convince the dog to allow itself to be restrained and handled *before* puberty, the chances of having the relationship develop into a positive experience are sharply reduced.

I've been working with pet owners for over seventeen years, and I can't recall a single, non-fear-related aggression case where a pet owner could restrain his or her pet against it's wishes! In the world of the wolf, subordination is a must, or pack members would continually act impulsively, and chaos would reign. The juveniles are pinned to the ground by older packs members before their fourth month! It is a natural developmental stage that canines pass through. The family dog is no exception. They all must be properly subordinated if they are to develop their potentials as super family dogs!

We tell NUPOs to practice subordination at least five times a day between now and the next class meeting. We caution them to make sure the Take-Down is gentle and causes *no* discomfort. If they twist the pup when taking it down, the pup might react defensively and resist in order to prevent pain.

Not for Discipline

The Take-Down is NOT USED FOR DISCIPLINE. Unlike wolves, NUPOs are simply not able to do it smoothly and quickly enough for it to be effective. Their goal is to build trust and respect so that they can place the pup on its side and keep it there until they release it.

After Waldo no longer tries to get up, Mom and Dad are asked to hold each paw for a ten count, put a finger in an ear, open the mouth and examine the teeth and gums, and examine the eyes and groin area. Next class we'll be showing them how to introduce brushing so that the puppy learns to enjoy rather than fight, it. This handling is preparation for next week's session and for nail clipping and ear and teeth cleaning on the Third Puppy Night.

Alternate Methods

If we have a pup that will not settle in the Subordinate position after several attempts, we work with the dog and its owner individually after class. Some very young and emotional puppies are not able to tolerate restraint for any longer than a few seconds. If this is the problem, we have the owner sit and hold the pup on his or her lap, then place the dog on its side for several *seconds* before releasing. They're asked to build up the time gradually over the coming week.

Some pups act afraid when restrained on the ground and struggle because of apprehension. If this is the case, we have the owner try placing the pup on its side on the bench or across the lap. Others may be apprehensive simply because this is the first night of class and there are strange pups and people nearby. In this case, a week of getting used to subordination at home should solve the problem.

Then there's Waldo. He doesn't want to be quiet for two minutes, but it's not because he's too young. When he's home and stalking ground squirrels, he's able to freeze for minutes on end. And it's not because he's afraid, because he hits the deck like he's a potted plant every time the neighbor's wolfhound gets within two yards! No, the reason Waldo isn't cooperating is because he just doesn't want to. It's up to Mom and Dad to convince him it's in his best interest to do so.

Some Moms and Dads are not emotionally capable of having it out with him. If this is the case, we feel it's best not to push them. And they're cautioned not to attempt to try to subordinate unless they're prepared to go all the way. Once Waldo learns they can't prevent him from getting up, he'll just become more determined, so it's best he doesn't discover their inability. Most NUPOs who have difficulty subordinating the first night, are able to come back to it before the class graduates. It just takes some people longer to "get up" for the confrontation when they have a Waldo.

Handing out the homework officially concludes First Puppy Night. If there are NUPOs with additional questions, we ask them to remain after class so we can answer them individually.

SECOND PUPPY NIGHT

Most dogs return to the Second SuperPuppy Class night with a marked change in attitude, and the NUPOs usually arrive early, eager to begin. If all the homework has been done, the pups enter class appearing more at ease, and excitedly greet the puppies and people they met last session.

At this class meeting we'll cover:

1. A review and test of Controlled Walking.

2. The next level of Controlled Walking.

3. An introduction to the off-leash Recall.

4. A review of subordination.

5. How to induce a relaxation response before brushing.

6. A demonstration of what to do when a pup mouths, nips, and/or jumps up on its NUPO.

7. A discussion of any problems that occur while the NUPO is away from home or the pup is unsupervised.

"Father Time"

The first thing we tell the class is that tonight they're going to get a pop quiz, but it's going to be an extremely fair test as we're going to give out the answers beforehand!

Nancy demonstrates the Controlled Walking procedure several times and asks for questions. We then ask them to come out and practice Controlled Walking, and when they're ready, they can take the test by simply walking past one of us.

If we feel a NUPO doesn't need any more review, we ask him or her to have a seat after giving plenty of praise! Those that need more coaching are kept practicing with our help and encouragement.

We call the training test "Father Time," because NUPOs have been known to grow old and weary waiting to sit down! In fact, I ask them if they remember seeing a student from Monday's class working on Controlled Walking when they arrived!

We really like "Father Time" as it's a fun way to get NUPOs to concentrate on what they're doing. Most of the time when someone is having trouble executing properly, it's because he or she didn't read and practice the homework. The "Father Time" test encourages them to do better next time because one thing a normal, healthy NUPO doesn't want to be is one of the last to sit down!

Slow Learners and Stubborn Students

If someone is having problems because he or she isn't able to coordinate their Teaching Actions just right, we can work privately with them after class. We just ask him or her to have a seat for now.

If a student wants to do Controlled Walking his or her own way and ignores the instructions, we let that person go on and on. By this time everyone else is seated watching the show. Many times this will make them more receptive to suggestions!

From time to time we have someone enroll who will persistently continue to teach his or her own way. After we make several attempts to help, we simply ask whether or not he or she wants our feedback.

Unless what they're doing is disruptive to the class or abusive or unfair to the pup, we'll leave such a student alone. I think it's important to be up front about this because, if you're a teacher, you know how frustrating it is to try to teach someone who isn't receptive!

Keep-Away

After everyone is seated, Nancy demonstrates the next level of Controlled Walking. We call it Keep-Away. Those people who have pups that are paying good attention during Controlled Walking will be ready for Keep-Away.

Keep-Away is a training game that is played to a score of ten. Whenever the NUPO makes a change in direction, speed, or both, and the pup compensates, the pup scores a point. If the pup receives a leash pop because it isn't paying attention and misses a change, the NUPO scores a point. After a total of ten points are scored, a Time Out is called.

We tell them that unless the pup's scoring seven or more of the possible points, they're not ready for Keep-Away. If they're not ready, they should continue to teach Controlled Walking at the introductory level.

We also ask them not to play the game all the time during their Controlled Walking sessions, but only once or twice. It doesn't replace Controlled Walking as introduced First Puppy Night, but is a way of making it more challenging and fun.

Introducing the Recall

The next item of business is introducing the Recall. I ask for a show of hands of who would like to teach their dog to come when called as if shot from a cannon and then slide into an automatic sit at their feet. Without hesitation all hands fly up. (Conformation dogs can be taught to come, stand, and bait.)

I tell them, "Starting with tonight's class and continuing throughout the rest of the meetings, we'll be working intensively on the Recall. But before we start, we need to discuss the reasons many people fail to teach a reliable Recall.

Building Trust

"In order for the dog to respond without hesitation, it must totally trust that coming will *not* lead to immediate unpleasant consequences. This means that you must *never* call your dog and then do something it doesn't like. Since dogs have individual preferences, likes and dislikes will differ.

"For example, some pups do not like to be bathed, but others love to get wet. If you have a dog that doesn't care for a bath, don't call him over and immediately throw him in the tub! He'll quickly learn not to trust your call.

"Get to know your pups' preferences now. Be aware of those things that bother them, and make sure you don't do any of them immediately after your pups come to you!"

Then I ask them to name some of the things their pups object to. Included in their replies are things like taking medication, nail clipping, flea spray, car riding, being put somewhere alone, going to the veterinarian, and grooming.

Adding a Delay

I tell the NUPO's that when they have to do something the dog doesn't care for, all they need to do, provided they do not forecast what's about to take place, is to call the pup over and then postpone the unpleasantness by *immediately* doing something the pup finds rewarding, such as playing ball, doing tricks, or giving tummy rubs. If they just wait a minute or two, then do what they have to do, the pups will not associate the act of coming with the unpleasant state of affairs that follows!

"If you don't have the bath water running while holding the brush in one hand and the shampoo in the other, they'll continue to come even though coming was eventually followed by the hated bath!"

Major Training Errors

Probably the worst mistake a NUPO or anyone can make is to call a dog over for discipline! No puppy in its right mind is going to trust a human who does that to them!

The other common error is to call repeatedly and then, getting no response, resort to a series of coaxing actions that deteriorates to pleading, begging, and bribing or escalates to screaming, yelling, and chasing!

Body Awareness

Next I ask each NUPO to show us how he or she presently calls the puppy. They usually say something like, "Wanda, here," but forget what they do with their bodies. Once I remind them how important body language is, they remember clapping their hands, crouching down, patting their legs, opening their arms wide, or bending over.

Informal vs. Formal Recall

I tell them, "You can continue to call your puppies just as you are now doing. We'll refer to this as the 'Informal Recall.' The way we're going to teach you how to do it will be a 'Formal Recall,' and will involve a specific hand signal and body posture. Also, we'll be suggesting a brand new verbal call, one that hasn't been associated with any bad habits."

Sit on Signal

Nancy then demonstrates the first step of the Recall. She will teach a pup to Sit on a hand signal. The signal we use is a movement of the right hand to the left shoulder. (If they prefer, conformation students are shown how to signal and shape the Stand.)

She doesn't say "sit," because we want the pup to learn that when it's called, it should come and sit *automatically*. She does three repetitions, then chooses another pup and does three more. She then returns to the first pup. Because of the Time Out, the pup usually sits immediately without prompting.

Shaping

We ask for questions and make sure that everyone knows how to shape the Sit without causing the pup any confusion or discomfort. Many NUPOs will try to make the pup sit by pushing down on the spine. This could be very uncomfortable and possibly harmful.

If a pup doesn't sit right away, the NUPO is shown how to shape it *gently* into a Sit by first hooking one finger under the collar using the leash hand while the other hand *tucks* the rump into the Sit. The pup is shown the Sit hand signal once more, then rewarded with a treat. The treat is placed into the signal hand *before* starting. (See the SuperPuppy Class II Homework handout for an illustration of the shaping procedure.)

Pause After Sitting

The pup is held in the Sit for five seconds. The NUPOs are asked to find a special place that their pups like to be touched and petted and to spend a few seconds loving them up. We explain that when the dogs get older, they'll no longer need a food reward for coming, but will *always* need to be petted and praised

The reason we want them to wait five seconds is to ensure that, after the pups come and sit, they do not immediately pop up and run off, but pause so that the owner can put on the leash, take hold of the collar, pick up the pup, or signal the Finish!

We then ask everyone to bring their dog out and do three Sits in a row. After a Time Out, they do three more. We have the NUPOs who aren't having any problems take a seat and work individually with the NUPOs who are having difficulty executing.

Add the Approach

The next step is to teach the pup to come over and Sit on hand signal and praise alone. At this point *no* verbal Recall is used.

The reason we don't have the NUPOs call their pups verbally is because we want to be sure that the pups fully understand the meaning of the hand signals before we add the verbal. If they do, then the *first* time they hear the call, it will be unambiguous. It will be combined with signals that are *already* associated with proper performance, rather than the confusion that occurs when NUPOs are learning something new!

Without knowing it, the NUPOs have already been working on teaching the pups to approach quickly on signal! For a week they've been signaling Time Out at the end of a Controlled Walking teaching segment. When they made the "smack-smack" sound and dropped down to reward the pups at the end of a Controlled Walking segment, the dogs learned to come over quickly to receive praise, petting, and a food reward.

Recall Hand Signal

We take advantage of this prior learning by having the NUPOs say the dog's name, follow with the "smack-smack" sound, and quickly move back several yards while praising and giving the Recall hand signal. The Recall hand signal is given by stretching the arm out to the side and then making a "come hither" motion to the chest. It's repeated continuously as the pup comes. The NUPOs then drop down, *still praising*, and when the pup arrives, give the hand signal for Sit. Praise continues through the five second delay.

Individual Attention

After the demonstration and questions and answers, we ask them to practice by themselves, doing two sets of three repetitions with a Time Out in between. We then divide into the Teaching Groups and work with everyone individually. Most NUPOs will be able to remain standing after signaling their puppies to approach on the six-foot leash by the time this session is finished.

Adding the Verbal

We ask them to spend at least *three* days perfecting the Recall and Sit hand signals. The next step is to add the verbal call. We suggest they use "Front" because, for most people and dogs, it's new, so it hasn't been associated with noncompliance or acquired negative connotations. At this point, they can also drop out the "smack-smack" sound.

Their goal for the next class meeting is to teach the pups to come quickly on *one* "Front," while holding the leash and standing upright. In order for the pups to learn the lesson reliably, it *must* be practiced under distraction and in different locations away from home.

Adding Distractions

Once the puppy is coming consistently and sitting automatically (usually about two to three days of practice), we ask them to go "looking for trouble!" We want them to place the pup in distracting circumstances so, when it doesn't respond to the call, they can pop the leash for attention as they did in the Controlled Walking exercise.

We remind them *never* to repeat the verbal command, and *never* to say "No" or raise their voices if the pup doesn't respond.

Keep the Training Equipment On

We ask them *never, ever* to call their pups using "Front" and the Front hand signal unless the dogs are *on the training equipment*, which is either a six-foot leash or the light lines that will be provided at the two next class meetings.

We tell them that if they've been successful in teaching the Front on leash, next week they'll be ready to learn how to use the ten-foot light training line. In the meantime, at this stage of the training, we strongly suggest that the puppies not be allowed to run free unless they're in a safe and securely fenced area. Then, if they need to call their pups, they should use the informal Recall.

I tell them, "The reason for not using Front unless the pups are on training equipment, is to ensure immediate compliance to the request. All it would take, at this stage of learning, would be *one* uncorrected hesitation or refusal, and the Front would be in danger of becoming unreliable."

After questions and answers we take a five to ten minute water break, then continue Second Puppy Night with discussion of subordination, mouthing, jumping up, brushing, and problem solving in Group.

Second Half

The second half of Second Puppy Night is taught in the Groups. We begin by asking everyone to report on their progress or problems. Usually, those NUPOs who are still having some problems with their pups' behavior while they're *home* with the dogs have not yet established a reliable Stop command. In order to help work out any difficulties, I ask them to explain, in detail, how they are attempting to handle a typical problem.

Detailed Explanation

Although it takes time, I feel it's best to have someone with a problem describe it in detail. This helps other NUPOs in the Group as they can compare and contrast the presented problem to their own situation. They may not have this particular difficulty now, but may face it, or a similar one, in the future.

It also starts them thinking about behavior problems analytically. One of the goals of SuperPuppy Class is to teach NUPOs how to break down a behavior problem in order to arrive at solutions that work.

Asking Questions

A typical exchange may go something like this: "Waldo is doing okay walking on the leash, but I'm still having trouble with him chasing and jumping on our four-year-old daughter, Christy."

The first thing I'd like to have is a description of a typical incident involving "daughter dumping."

"Could you tell us about the last time this happened?" "Yes, it was right before we came to class. Waldo and Christy were out in the back yard playing while I was getting ready to load everyone into the car. Christy came running into the house, crying, and when I asked what happened, she said Waldo jumped up and knocked her down."

"Is that all that she said?"

"No, she also told me later, after she stopped crying, that she doesn't always like Waldo and wanted to know if he's going to live with us forever."

I know from the enrollment form that Christy is the only child. I also know that four-year-olds play politics. If Christy doesn't want to share Mommy with anyone, she may very well lobby to remove Waldo from the scene, especially if he's not the cuddly "stuffed toy" she thought a puppy would be.

But Christy also has a legitimate complaint. Waldo is a very active young tiger who plays rough 'n tumble. Can the two positions be reconciled — Christy's ambivalence toward the dog, and Waldo's need for some flat-out fun?

Toddlers Can't Train

We can rule out having Christy teach Waldo not to jump on her. She simply isn't mentally, emotionally, or physically able to do this. If we suggest that Mom teach Waldo not to jump on Christy, then Mom would need to be present when the two interact.

In many situations involving pups and children, I feel this should be the recommendation. The *child* may tend to be too rough, and the pup sensitive, or vice versa. Many other different combinations of personalities and temperaments might call for close parental supervision. But in this particular situation, isn't there a way to have the dog and the child happily together for short, unsupervised moments?

Does the Stop Command Work?

Before I rush in with suggestions, I want to know if Mom's been able to teach Waldo to "stop and report in," using the beanbag and raised voice technique described last week.

"Can you get him to stop jumping on Christy when you're around?" If the answer is no, then we have to find out why not.

"Have you tried?"

"Yes, but he doesn't listen to me."

"Could you describe exactly what you tried in order to control the jumping?"

"I've repeatedly told him to 'stop it,' and pushed him off Christy."

Now I have something I can work with — a *description* of a Teaching Action that was ineffective. My next question is, "Did you use your beanbag?"

"Yes, but sometimes it isn't handy."

Now I can re-explain the importance of *always* having the beanbag in the pocket, along with training treats, during the first two weeks of teaching good manners. Also, I can re-emphasize the importance of not talking to the pup when teaching. Instead of saying "stop it" and pushing the dog off, I can remind Mom to toss the beanbag and say "Erhhh" when the beanbag lands and then immediately pet, praise, and reward Waldo.

Indirect Interaction

Next, I'll focus on why Waldo chases and jumps up on Christy. It's no big mystery — that's how pups play with each other. They chase and dump each other all day long. Waldo's playing with Christy the only way he knows how! He's acting as if Christy were a two-legged, upright-running, funny-smelling puppy!

Can he be taught otherwise? Certainly! What will be required though, is for Christy to learn not to play with him directly, but *indirectly*, using an object with which they can both interact.

Choosing Play Objects

Play objects are best chosen from those things in which the pup naturally seems interested. The last time we had our two-year old grandson over, he played ball with our gang until *he* got tired of the game, about 10 minutes! If the puppy's not interested in a ball, it might get a kick out of throwing around and carrying an empty, plastic, gallon water bottle, pushing a soccer ball, or another safe item. I'll suggest that Mom find objects that Waldo and Christy can't easily use for tug-of-war as that type of game might encourage roughhousing.

Play Retrieving Solves Problems

I'll also suggest Mom work with Christy and Waldo by teaching them play retrieving using three items, as outlined in the *SuperPuppy* book. We've found if NUPOs follow the play retrieve procedure *exactly*, it usually takes about two weeks to get a young dog "hooked" on the game!

I'll suggest she give this a try and report back next week or call during the week if she has difficulty. If Christy learns to play retrieve with Waldo, and Mom teaches her *never* to chase, hit, or throw things at him, and NEVER to tease him by making believe she threw something or by hiding the item behind her back, Waldo will have no *reason* to jump up on Christy. Not only that, but the child will become someone special in his life — someone who provides the opportunity to express an important young dog need — maniacal running!

Introducing Brushing

Next on the agenda is to show NUPOs how to introduce brushing. This will also give us an opportunity to review the take-down and subordination procedure.

We ask the NUPOs to place their pups into the subordinate position. They should wind up directly behind the pups with one hand on the neck scruff. (See the illustration under "Restrain for Ten Seconds" in the "First Puppy Night" chapter.) Next they're asked to pick up their brushes, and using either the *back* of the brush or the brush *handle* (if they have a two-sided brush), begin slowly stroking and softly praising their dogs. If they are gentle, talk softly, and use light pressure on the brush, and have been successful with the subordination exercises, after about two to three minutes an amazing thing begins to happen — the pups start to *close their eyes!*

Inducing a Relaxation Response

We explain to them that what they're doing is inducing a relaxation response. If we were to measure the dogs' brain waves after the eyes close, we'd see a marked change to brain wave pattern associated with relaxation!

We tell them, "Once your dog starts to close its eyes, you can begin to turn the brush over and use the bristle side, but only do so briefly, then return to the smooth side. If you use too much pressure, go too fast, or pull the coat, they'll open their eyes, so watch their eyes to see how you're doing."

Grooming in the Wild

We tell them, "Healthy, wild canines regularly practice mutual grooming. This is usually done at least once a day and seems to be a important part of pack life. When you think about it, their coats are essential for survival. Not only does each animal spend a good deal of time grooming itself, but grooms others as well. If the coat isn't kept in top shape, health problems may ensue, and the animal could be at risk as far as survival is concerned.

"They spend a great deal of time preventing problems by keeping the coat clean and the parasite population in check. They also appear to enjoy mutual grooming, so the behavior may have social, as well as health, implications.

Reasons for Brushing

"One of the best things you can do to keep your dog clean, healthy, and attractive is regular *daily* brushing."

Many new pet owners think bathing is the only way to clean the pup, but too frequent bathing may be detrimental to coat and skin health. We tell them how brushing not only removes dirt and debris from the coat, but stimulates the natural skin oils and activates the immune system.

We feel that every NUPO should be able to handle the pup for brushing, even if they have it groomed professionally. The pup should be brushed daily and have enough trust and respect for it's owner to allow this to happen. Most pups will come to enjoy brushing if it's introduced carefully, but even if they don't beg to be brushed, the pups are making a strong, positive statement about the developing dog/human relationship when they relax and don't struggle.

We then ask for questions about grooming in general and ask if they have questions about skin and coat care, including parasite identification and control.

Diet

We are also prepared to talk about diet and diet management at this time. Since this is a highly disputed area, we only discuss it if a NUPO brings it up. We describe the various positions taken by pet food companies, veterinarians, breeders, trainers, and independent nutritionists, and stress the importance of feeding a high quality, nutritionally complete puppy food. Since what to feed puppies, and dogs in general, is so controversial, we tell NUPOs that it's best to decide what to do after researching the question themselves.

I'm sure that some of you will feel this is a "cop out," but since no one brand of food or dietary regimen seems to work equally well for all dogs and puppies, we are very conservative about this issue in our class.

Although I'm sure some common behavior problems are influenced by diet, my experience tells me that changing the diet alone, without making any other changes, will probably not change the objectionable behavior. If a pup has obvious problems that may be diet-related, such as over- or underweight, dry coat, low energy, or coprophagia, we suggest bringing it up with their vet, as such symptoms may have additional causes.

Close Secluded Confinement

The next topic for Group concerns problems that may be occurring while the pup is unattended and Mom and Dad are away from home.

Like many of you, we've been preaching to NUPOs for years about the necessity for using close, secluded confinement when the pup is unattended. In SuperPuppy Class, about half of the NUPOs try either the crate or the crate and exercise pen as part of their puppy rearing procedure!

This is probably due to the integrated approach that is used. The Orientation introduces the concept, presenting it as coming from the dog's natural den dwelling inclinations. The *SuperPuppy* book reinforces this argument, and class work emphasizing the need for immediate feedback in teaching dogs removes delayed punishment as a viable way of dealing with misbehavior occurring during an absence.

Not Forever

I tell them, "The best way I know to raise a pup and be able to leave it safely alone is to use secluded, close confinement. This is not for the rest of their lives. It is a *temporary* measure used when they're growing up. Once they're well trained and socialized adults, they'll be emotionally able to deal with separations, but until they mature, it's imperative to have them in a secluded, den-like environment when they cannot be supervised.

Beware of Frustrating Confinement

"A den is a dark, secluded place. If you were to pen them up outside, or put them in a crate outside, you would be doing something other than denning your pups. You would be placing them in a very vulnerable, frustrating position. They'd be constantly stimulated by the outside happenings, such as neighbors, cats, other dogs, loud noises, birds, delivery people, or meter readers. Because of confinement, the expression of appropriate responses to these stimuli would repeatedly be frustrated.

"If fearful, they could not run and hide. If teased by a neighbor's cat, they could not chase off the cat. If greeted by a friendly meter reader, they could not get out and play. Over the long term, frustrating conditions often lead to serious side effects, including debilitating fears or aggression, as well as destruction, excessive vocalization, and frantic escape attempts.

Seclusion is Necessary

"In order to ensure nothing like this happens to your puppy while it's growing up, find an *inside* area that you can make dark.

"Place your den and/or exercise pen in this area as outlined in your *SuperPuppy* books. Before you do this you must introduce them properly to the devices. It will take two days of training, following the training procedure in your books. Once den trained, the pup will readily enter the area, be calm and quiet, and will usually sleep during your shorter absences.

"If you're gone more than three or four hours at any one time, you'll need an exercise pen. This will allow the pup to eliminate, play with safe toys, and drink.

"In nature, dens are naturally soundproof. Instead of soundproofing a spare room, all you need do is turn on an FM radio moderately loud to an 'elevator music' station. This acts as a buffer to incoming auditory stimulation. Remember, your goal is to block out stimulation as best you can, and believe me, elevator music is not stimulating by itself — it will put almost anyone to sleep!"

The "Rent-A-Den" Plan

As an inducement for them to use close, secluded confinement, I would strongly suggest that puppy classes provide a crate and pen rental/purchase plan for NUPOs . A nonprofit organization, such as a dog club, could easily offer the equipment at cost, so NUPOs would be able to rent or buy for considerably less than retail.

If several dog clubs, humane societies, or other sponsoring organizations combine on ordering the equipment, an even greater savings can be passed on to NUPOs . I feel this would help remove the last valid objection that NUPOs have for not using close, secluded confinement — the considerable cost of quality denning equipment.

Creative Booby Trapping

Often, older puppies and young adults who show no signs of stress begin to do things that their owners object to when they are left alone. We suggest that NUPOs gradually allow their young dogs more and more freedom as they mature. If, however, they should get into trouble after they have clearly shown they can handle being alone, there is still a way — we show them how to rig an effective but harmless booby trap!

Booby trapping is *never*, *ever* recommended for immature dogs who are presenting problems while alone. It could easily make things worse by intensifying the stress produced through loneliness, or create stress where none was present!

It is used to discourage those behaviors that are best characterized as mischievous or recreational! Here's a typical example, using our blue Sheltie, Kis:

Nancy and I had just finished putting in a rock garden in the backyard. We labored all weekend, and as the final touch, I installed an automatic watering system using flexible, plastic pipe. The pipe was buried underground and supplied each plant with water through drip emitters. It was a work of art!

Kis was just over a year old, and we often gave her the run of the house and yard. I had to run to the hardware store to pick up some last minute gardening supplies, and without thinking twice, got in the car and left. I was only gone thirty minutes — more than enough time for her to dig up half of the pipe and chew it to shreds!

Several hours later everything was back in order and working well, but I knew she'd probably try it again. After all, killing plastic pipe is something most blue swamp collies are bred to do, right?

...and Kis was leading the retreat!

In any event, I didn't want to take the chance that she'd continue to frustrate and anger me by digging up and destroying my masterpiece. My job was to convince her that plastic pipe is *trouble*. Since Kis hated the sound of the shaker can, I knew that if the pipe could "toss" the can the instant she grabbed it, she'd gain new respect for the object of Dad's backbreaking labor!

The booby trap used in this situation was a shaker can that would be catapulted through the air by a rat trap. A six-pound test, nylon monofilament fishing line was tied to several plastic water pipes of various sizes, and then tied to the bait plate of the rat trap.

The rat trap was placed in the crotch of nearby tree and nailed down so it could not move. After *carefully* setting the trap, a shaker can, flattened on one side, was *gently* lowered onto it. After the booby trap was complete, I brought Kis out, and as we approached the garden, I picked up the pipe and purposely set the trap off!

Everything worked perfectly. The trap went off, tossing the can in our direction. I took off like someone was throwing live grenades from next door, and Kis was leading the retreat.

The reason I set off the trap myself was to make sure everything was working, and to prepare Kis for the possibility that the pipe could be "dangerous." THE LAST THING I WOULD WANT WOULD BE FOR HER TO BE SO STARTLED BY THE BOOBY TRAP THAT SHE PAN-ICKED AND INJURED HERSELF TRYING TO GET AWAY, OR BE SO AFRAID THAT SHE WOULDN'T WANT TO GO INTO THE YARD AGAIN.

I left the trap up for five weeks, because she proved to be one determined little Sheltie. She set it off *three* times before giving up. Surely a new swamp collie record!

The important points to remember about successful booby trapping are:

1. *Never* use the procedure if the dog is emotionally immature.

2. *Never* use if the dog is in a state of stress or is temperamentally timid.

3. If using a shaker can, first make sure the dog is sensitized to its sound, using the method described under "Shaker Can Teaching Action" in the First Puppy Night chapter.

4. With the dog present, set off the device yourself and act startled. Reassure the dog that you had nothing to do with what happened. "It must have been that baaaad old rotten pipe!"

5. When setting up the booby trap, make sure the dog cannot readily detect that there has been a change in the environment.

6. *Never* place a rat trap where anyone can be injured by it.

7. To make sure the mischievous behavior will always be corrected, leave the booby trap set up for two to six weeks.

Jumping Up and Mouthing

The final discussion concerns what to do when Waldo jumps up on NUPO's or mouths on their hands or clothing. We wait until Second Puppy Night to talk about these problems because we want the NUPOs to have one week of subordination practice before attempting these procedures.

For mouthing, we suggest that they try over and over to get the pup to nip or mouth on their hands. As soon as the pup takes their hand with uncomfortable pressure, they are instructed to say, "Erhhh," and shake the neck scruff firmly with the other hand. When the pup releases the hand, the NUPO should immediately pet and praise.

We strongly suggest that NUPOs never play hand games with their pups. They should use a play item or retrieving toy that Waldo can mouth all he wants.

For jumping up on them, we demonstrate the procedure in the *SuperPuppy* book and answer questions. This method teaches a hand signal that comes to mean "no jump." The NUPO only needs to remember to show the hand signal to the pup *before* it approaches closer than three feet. Using this method, we've found that it takes about two to three weeks before most pups stop jumping up altogether.

After final questions and answers, we hand out the homework and give them a giant pep talk on how well they are doing and exhort them to keep it up and *do their homework!* Next week we'll cover nail clipping, ear cleaning, dental care, and other basic health matters, further work on Controlled Walking, and introduce a very important piece of equipment — the light training line.

FRONT on the six-foot leash.

THIRD PUPPY NIGHT

By the third meeting with the puppies, Controlled Walking is usually going very well for most NUPOs. We start things off having everyone "go for a walk." During the Time Outs we have the pups greet each other while the NUPOs hold them in the Greeting Position.

The Warm-Up

To get things going, I try to play appropriate tapes on the boom-box. Great training tunes such as *Hound Dog, A Dog Named Blue, Doggie In The Window,* and *Bird Dog* help get everyone moving about in a good mood.

After the warm-up we have the NUPOs take a seat and put their pups in the listening position. I ask if anyone has any questions about Controlled Walking. If we can't answer a question or solve a problem quickly, we ask the NUPOs who are still having some difficulty to see us after class for personalized pointers.

One-Handed Walking

Nancy then demonstrates the next level of Controlled Walking which we call One-Handed Walking. We tell them to do this *only* if they have good attention when playing "Keep-Away." Before beginning, Nancy demonstrates how to gather up one to two feet of the leash and hold it in the right hand. She then slaps her left side with her left hand, says, "Waldo, let's go for a walk," and moves off praising. Right *before* she makes a change in direction or pace, she again slaps her left leg. I tell them, "The reason we want to signal a forthcoming change by slapping the *left* leg is twofold: First, it helps to maintain attention by warning the pup that, unless it attends, a leash pop will follow. Second, it's the next step toward Heeling.

Left-Sided Walking

"Convention has it that the dog heels on the handler's left. By emphasizing this side early in the pup's training, those of you interested in obedience competition will have an easier time teaching formal Heeling later on.

It's also very convenient for everyday walking not to have the dog crossing back and forth in front of you.

"If you're going to go on to competition, you'll want to make sure that you always position *yourself* on your pup's right side when doing Controlled Walking. In other words, at this point, don't *demand* that the dog walk on your left; just make sure you're always on the right."

Practice Fronts

After questions and answers on Controlled Walking, we review the Fronts. First we re-demonstrate the exercise. Next, the class is divided into the Teaching Groups to make sure that everyone is executing well. We work individually with each student, focus on problem areas, and make sure to praise the NUPOs who are doing a good job.

Things to Look For

At this time, the pups should be coming quickly and sitting automatically while on leash, and the NUPOs should be able to call them away from distractions with *one* Front command. Typically, NUPOs have to be reminded to praise all the time they're working the pups. Many have a tendency to teach silently. This may lead to loss of attention, lowered tail posture, and overall reduction in enthusiasm on everyone's part.

Another typical problem is ill-timed, or unclear, hand signals. This, coupled with a poorly timed and/or ineffective leash pop, causes many a dog to wonder how he ever wound up with this Bozo!

We also take this opportunity to work the pups under distraction by having the NUPOs do on-leash Fronts side by side and Front their pups away from each other when they're standing in a small circle. After working in Groups, we take a water break and then introduce the ten-foot light training line.

The Light Line

We use the light line as a bridge between on-leash and off-leash work. It's transition training equipment that allows *both* hands to be used as they would in off-leash work, and it allows the pup to be farther away from the trainer. Because of its strength and lightness, it is safe and can easily be phased out.

The ten-foot light line is made from one-eighth inch *braided* nylon cord and has a loop at one end and a bolt snap at the other. The loop end is slipped around a leash that has been tied around the NUPO's waist. (See the illustration in the Homework section at the end of this manual.)

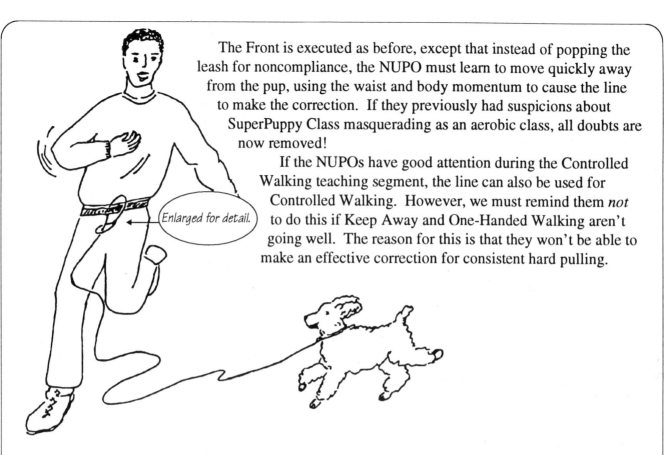

The Front is executed as before, except that instead of popping the leash for noncompliance, the NUPO must learn to move quickly away from the pup, using the waist and body momentum to cause the line to make the correction. If they previously had suspicions about SuperPuppy Class masquerading as an aerobic class, all doubts are now removed!

If the NUPOs have good attention during the Controlled Walking teaching segment, the line can also be used for Controlled Walking. However, we must remind them *not* to do this if Keep Away and One-Handed Walking aren't going well. The reason for this is that they won't be able to make an effective correction for consistent hard pulling.

Enlarged for detail.

Some Drawbacks

There are several problems involved with using ten feet of one-eighth inch nylon line. It can easily get underfoot (both the pup's and NUPOs), so care must be taken to prevent tripping and tangling. Another problem can be rope burn. When first using the line some NUPOs may try to correct by jerking the line with their hands. We suggest they wear gloves if they find themselves doing this, especially if they have a larger puppy!

We don't have the NUPOs use the line at class, because we've found that sixteen people walking around with their pups attached to their waists by ten feet of "spaghetti" can quickly turn into a giant macrame mess!

In SuperPuppy Class, we provide both the ten-foot light line which is given out at Third Puppy Night and the fifty-foot line which is given out at the following class. We've found that the NUPOs are most likely to complete this crucial part of recall training if they have the training equipment in their hands when they leave class!

"Waldo, Wait"

The next lesson is to teach the NUPOs how to teach their puppies to Wait until released. We suggest they *not* use the word "stay" for several reasons. Usually they have already told their pups to "stay" meaning "stay in the kitchen," "stay in the car," or "stay in the yard." Also, we still haven't met the puppy who really listens when "taught" to Stay by a NUPO. I tell them, "The reason we use the word "Wait" at SuperPuppy Class is to give you a fresh start and to emphasize that the command must come to mean to the pup: 'Don't move from the *position* you're in until you're released.'''

The Practical Side

"This is a very important lesson for your pups to learn, as the command can be used daily. For example, once it's trained up, the Wait will give you control if you drop a dish in the kitchen; give grandma a chance to get in the front door without a being hassled, visit peacefully, and eat in peace; or allow you to complete a task without interruption.

"It's also good for the pups to begin to learn to control their impulses. Part of growing up involves learning not always to act impulsively. Although they're much too young to be expected to Wait for an extended period of time, they're not too young to learn not to move for a minute or two. This is all we're going to ask of them at first. By the end of the week they should be able to Wait while distracted without moving for *one* minute."

Waits in Real Life

I have two stories I tell about how former students used the Wait in real life situations. The first is about our friend Bill Anderson and his Doberman, Misty, now a CDX and member of San Diego County Search and Rescue! Bill is a sailor, and he and Misty were cruising off San Diego on Bill's sailboat. Just the two of them were aboard, and at that time Misty was still in SuperPuppy Class. Bill reports that suddenly a problem developed with the rigging which required his immediate attention. True to puppy form, Misty was doing everything she could to "help Bill out." Things were going nowhere fast until Bill remembered the Wait! Bill told us that to his amazement he was then able to take care of the problem, unassisted.

The second story is a tale told by Harry Langman about his Samoyed, Dudley. Now Dudley was one active reindeer router, but as is often the case with overly active dogs, he had no trouble learning to Wait. In fact, Harry claims that one particular morning Dudley was "helping" him pack for a business trip. Unfortunately, his help went unappreciated as Harry was running late for the drive to the airport. After repeatedly asking Dudley to stop bothering him, Harry reports that out of desperation, he put Dudley on a Wait, quickly finished packing, grabbed the suitcases, and flew out the front door. Halfway to the airport he remembered that he hadn't released Dudley from the Wait! As soon as he could get to a phone, he called his wife, Pat, and asked her if she'd seen Dudley. You guessed it. Harry says that the dog was still on a Down Wait when Pat checked the bedroom!

Don't Say "Sit"

We begin to teach the Wait from a shaped Sit. I tell them, "The first step is to *put* your pups into a Sit and gather up the leash. It's important for them think they are *free* to move, so make sure they cannot feel any tension from the leash. It's much easier for them to learn a reliable Wait if they feel they are *not* being held in place, but are free to leave the Sit. Do not say 'sit.' Just gently place them in that position, say 'wait,' and extend the open palm of your hand toward them as a hand signal. The reason we don't want you to say 'sit' is because we want *you*, as well as the pups, to concentrate upon one thing only - not *leaving* the Sit position without being corrected.

Fast Feedback Critical

"As soon as they begin to stand or lie down, say, "Erhhh," and jerk the leash. Then, *immediately* and softly, praise and gently pet. The reason for this is to reassure them you're not upset — it was just the fact that they attempted to leave the Sit that caused the commotion. If you're *late* with the correction, DON'T DO ANYTHING; just reposition and try again.

Don't Jerk Into the Sit

"The reason for jerking on the leash is to provide Fast Feedback for leaving the Sit, *not* to put them back into it. So only correct *once*, then TAKE YOUR TIME and gently replace them. The *only* time you have to hurry is the *instant* they attempt to

NUPO teaching the Sit/Wait.

leave the Sit. The reason for raising your voice is to pair your raised voice with the leash pop so that your voice will be effective feedback when you're no longer holding the leash.

Clear Release

"Count quietly to five and release. On the release, make the 'smack-smack' sound, give the Front hand signal, and run back ten feet, praising. When the pup arrives, show the Sit hand signal and reward with food, continue to praise, and then pet. Take the food out of your pocket as you run back.

Starting From the Sit

"The reason we start teaching the Wait while the pups are *seated* is because experience has shown it's the easiest position from which to learn. From an everyday, practical standpoint, the most stable position from which to ask them to Wait is the prone position. This is because it's probably a more comfortable position for them for longer periods of time. Next week we'll show you how to teach the Wait while Down, so practice regularly, and they'll be properly prepared."

Choose Active Demo Dogs

Nancy demonstrates the procedure with several pups. She tries to choose dogs who are very active and don't mind working for her. After the demos we ask everyone to practice three in a row. I remind them what to do for the first set of three, then we take a Time Out from this exercise.

Vary the Walking

During the Time Out, we have the NUPOs practice Controlled Walking, but with a new twist. While they're walking, we call for them to do Keep-Away, One-handed Walking, and Quiet Walking, along with numerous pace and direction changes. Quiet Walking is Controlled Walking done for a short period without Happy Talk.

Wait Problems

We have the class practice three more Waits, and then ask those who are not having difficulty to take a seat. After working with the remaining NUPOs, we return to the benches and answer questions.

The most common problem is a late correction — the leash isn't popped until the puppy is up and walking away. We work carefully with NUPOs to correct this because if they continue to teach in that manner, a sensitive puppy will become confused and want to avoid the entire Wait exercise. A less sensitive pup simply won't learn. We also have to remind some NUPOs to raise their voices in combination with the leash pop so, later on, they'll be able to teach the Wait from a substantial distance.

Wait Increments

The homework on the Wait asks them to build up the Wait time gradually to one minute. The homework also asks them to begin to move around and away from the pup using very small increments so that, by the end of the week, they can move all the way around the pup holding the leash from up to five feet away. After two or three days, they must also begin to teach the Wait with distractions. By next class meeting, their goals are to have the puppy Wait for approximately *one* minute under distraction and to be able to walk all the way around the dog while it's Waiting.

Promoting Trust and Respect

The second half of Third Puppy Night is taught in Groups and consists of a hands-on workshop covering:

1. Handling the pup for nail clipping.
2. Ear cleaning.
3. Dental care.
4. Answering questions raised on general health care.
5. Answering remaining questions on at home behavior.

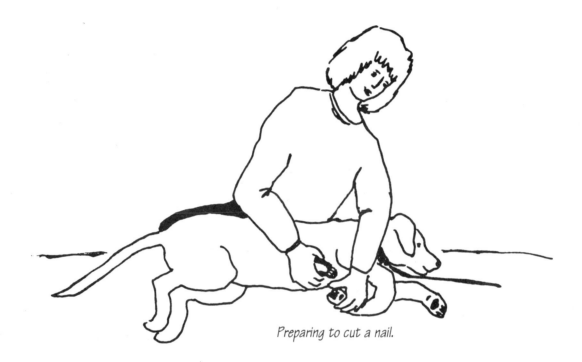

Preparing to cut a nail.

We feel that each NUPO should be able to handle the pup for the above grooming procedures even if they have them done professionally, as these handling procedures promote mutual trust and respect.

By allowing their owners to clip nails and clean ears and teeth, the pups are making a strong, positive statement about the relationship with their owners. By developing the ability and confidence to perform such tasks, NUPOs begin to transcend reservations they may have about close, intimate handling of another species — a transcendence crucial for true bonding to occur.

I tell them, "In all the years I've been working with dog owners, I can't recall a single instance involving non-fear related aggression toward the owner, where the pet owner was able to clip the dog's nails and clean the teeth and ears!"

Keep Them Enthusiastic

We've found that Third Puppy Night seems to be a turning point for many NUPOs and their pups. If they've kept up on their homework, they're eager to learn more and look forward to the remaining three weeks.

If, however, they've had to struggle to get the work in or are not satisfied with their progress, they may begin to lose motivation. We try to encourage them by saying, "If everyone makes a big effort to prepare the pups for the next class, we'll guarantee a great time for everyone!

"Next week we'll be introducing the first obstacles. The use of obstacles in puppy training is one big reason SuperPuppy Class is so different than a typical beginners' obedience class. If you do your homework and come to class fully prepared, we'll be able to show your how to do things you never dreamed you could get your puppies to do, like Front through a tunnel past other pups walking in their path!

"They'll also learn to run over a teeter totter and an inverted V-ramp. In the following weeks we'll have still other obstacles that will motivate them to perform while building their trust in you, and confidence in their own abilities to succeed in performing new and challenging activities. Next week really begins their journey toward becoming a true super puppy, so don't miss it! DO YOUR HOMEWORK!"

FOURTH PUPPY NIGHT

There are two SuperPuppy classes that we especially look forward to teaching. One is the Orientation and the other is Fourth Puppy Night. The Orientation is special because we begin to see people start to look differently at the task of raising a dog. Fourth Puppy Night is special because we begin to teach principles, not just procedures, and we introduce the dogs to obstacles. Our focus becomes much more positive as NUPOs can now concentrate on teaching their pups *to* do something instead of *not* to do something.

The first three classes, as well as the Orientation, were primarily concerned with not to's: teaching Waldo not to jump up, not to eliminate inside, not to chew destructively, not to struggle when being groomed, etc. Necessarily, a great deal of time was devoted to establishing a relationship based upon respect as well as affection and trust. In order to accomplish these ends, NUPOs needed to learn effective Teaching Actions that would cause the pup to stop whatever it was doing and report back to them.

At Fourth Puppy Night we begin to change the emphasis by concentrating on the to do's. The Fourth Puppy Night goals are:

1. Begin to teach NUPOs the basic principles that underlie puppy training.
2. Teach NUPOs the proper way to introduce their pups to obstacles.
3. Teach the pups to Front through a rigid, seven-foot tunnel, scale an inverted V-ramp, and walk across a stabilized teeter board.
4. Explain and demonstrate the use of the fifty-foot light training line.
5. Introduce the Wait in the Down position.
6. Forecast phasing out food rewards on the Front.

Memory Aid

We use a mnemonic to help NUPOs memorize teaching principles. I tell them, "What we're going to concentrate upon tonight are the basic principles that underlie teaching puppies. I'm going to start by telling you Three Fibs. The three greatest fibs in dog training are: 'Our Puppy Class enrollment check is in the mail;' 'We were busy last week, and didn't have time to work our dog;' and 'I don't understand why she won't do it now — she does it perfectly at home!'

"Now, I'd like you to remember the Three Fibs, but only the number 3 and letters F, I, and B. I'm really not kidding. Just remember what the letters stand for, and you'll remember how to teach your puppies any series of actions as well as how to introduce them to obstacles.

Three Repetitions

"'Three' stands for three in a row. When teaching, remember to do only three repetitions of any one lesson at a time. Then take a Time Out before repeating that lesson.

"If you work with your pups in this fashion, you'll increase the chances that they'll maintain their interest in the lesson. More importantly, it appears that frequent Time Outs promote learning in puppies. It's as if what they've just experienced needs time to become consolidated within the learning centers of the brain. You'll notice this right off if you have a good teaching procedure because, if you do three in a row and then take a break, the pups will perform better when you resume teaching that lesson.

Fast Feedback

"'F' stands for Fast Feedback. Remember to provide the pups continuous feedback for their actions. The *instant* they do something that even *approximates* the desired response, make it rewarding for them. Verbal praise and reassurance are usually the fastest rewarding feedbacks you can provide. Petting and food take more time, and may interrupt the flow of the lesson if not carefully planned beforehand.

"Corrective actions must occur the instant the pup does something inappropriate. When you're learning to train dogs, you have to learn to focus your concentration on exactly what they're doing and be able to provide the proper feedback, automatically, at the ideal instant. This skill will take time to develop, and will only arise after repeated practice on your part.

Incremental Training

"'I' stands for Increments. We want you to build up to the desired result in small steps or increments. Remember when you began teaching the Front? You didn't start off by calling the pups from 100 feet, did you? The first teaching increment was the Sit. Then you had them approach when you made the 'smack-smack' sound and squatted down while holding the leash. After some practice you began to stand up, and then you went to the next training increment which was the ten-foot distance on the light line. You'll gradually increase the distance, working up to Fronts from 100 feet away!

"The idea is to make the initial training increments as simple for the puppy as possible. You need to set it up so that they are quickly successful at the task. This quick, initial success allows them to receive an immediate reward — the fast, positive feedback that leads to increased attention and desire.

Backward Chaining

"'B' stands for Backward Chaining. When teaching pups a series of steps that forms a chain of behaviors, it's usually best to begin at the back of the chain. How you introduced the Front is again a good example of backward chaining. Remember, your goal was to have your pup come and Sit

Front. The last behavior link in this chain of actions is sitting for a count of five. This is where you began to teach the Front. You started at the back, or terminal end, of the chain of behaviors that constitutes coming when called. So, if you remember the Three Fibs, you'll be a much better puppy raiser, and that's no lie!

Use Three Fibs for Obstacles

"You'll also use the Three Fibs when teaching the pups to negotiate an obstacle. For example, one of your goals tonight is to teach them to come to you through a children's play tunnel. You'll notice the tunnel compresses in order to fit into its storage box. Now, using Three Fibs, what can you do to begin teaching them to Front through the tunnel?"

Interesting Answers

The list of replies is sometimes amusing. NUPOs have suggested everything from crawling through the tunnel with the pups while holding the leash between their teeth to having the pups watch as they crawl through the tunnel themselves! I usually have to remind them that dogs learn by doing. Then I ask, "What does the 'I' stands for in Three Fibs. Yes, that's right, Increments! Then what should the first Training Increment be? Remember we need to set it up so that Wanda is quickly successful. Yes, very good! All we need do is fold up the tunnel as if we're going to put it back into its box. Then Wanda only has to take one step, and she's halfway home. She's passed through the four inches of tunnel, which may be a little scary for her, but it happened quickly and she's rewarded immediately. Now she'll be less apprehensive and more willing on the second try."

Why Obstacles?

Someone always asks why we use obstacles in the first place. My answer is, "We use obstacles especially designed for puppies because they are fantastic teaching aids! They represent new and varied challenges to the dogs. If the obstacles are properly introduced and worked with, the dogs develop confidence in themselves and in you as their teachers. A confident, outgoing attitude about working with you is part of becoming a super puppy.

"Some of you have pups that are more bashful or cautious than others. You'll see these timid pups start to come out of their shells as they learn to negotiate the obstacles.

"Others have pups that act as if they're not thinking about what they're doing. They react quickly and impulsively. Obstacles will help them slow down and use their heads to solve the physical and mental challenges the various obstacles present.

"Other puppies in this class are easily bored with routine training. Obstacles challenge these quick learners to develop their abilities. ALL the dogs will benefit in one way or another, and, besides that, the obstacles will be a lot of *fun* for you, too!"

Preventing Problems

Some final words about using obstacles. In the interest of safety and good sportsmanship we ask everyone to not step or walk on the obstacles themselves, and we ask them to wait until the team using an obstacle is well clear before starting. We also ask them to hold the pups by their collars when first using an obstacle that is raised above the ground.

Finally, we ask them not to use food as a lure to entice the pups over an obstacle. There are times that we'll need do this with an especially cautious dog, but we've learned that luring pups causes them to concentrate upon the *food* instead of what they're doing. In most cases this is undesirable and produces unnecessary and unwanted expectations. It also diverts NUPOs away from the notion of incremental training as they almost always think they should lure the pup over the entire obstacle right off the bat!

Tunnel Introduction

Nancy and I help the NUPOs introduce their pups to the tunnel. We take great care to ensure that ALL the dogs are successful. Some of them may be very apprehensive. If this is the case, we do *lots* of repetitions at very short tunnel lengths. However, only three repetitions are done in a row, and then the puppy is given a Time Out.

Introducing the tunnel.

NUPO's position

We start by having a NUPO bring a pup out and give the leash to Nancy. If the pup is small, we ask the NUPO to pick it up and hand it to her. I hold the tunnel in its completely folded position and ask the NUPO to squat down about two feet from the tunnel opening.

Don't Call

When Nancy's ready, she asks the NUPO to use Happy Talk, the "smack-smack" sound, and the Recall hand signal to encourage the pup to step through. No verbal commands are given. The puppies are never called through the tunnel during the introduction. This goes back to our primary rule for establishing trust on the recall: *Never* call your dog into a situation that *it* may find unpleasant.

Tunnel Increments

We do this two more times, and I gradually lengthen the tunnel on each repetition. We've found that most pups will be going through the full six-foot tunnel length after only three repetitions!

Keeping Them Busy

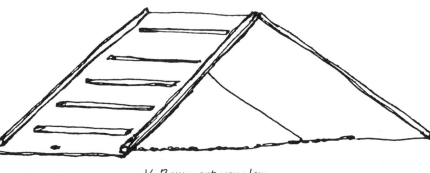

V–Ramp set very low.

While NUPOs are waiting their turns on the tunnel, we ask them to introduce their pups to two other obstacles, an inverted V-ramp set at its lowest position, and a teeter board that has been stabilized to prevent movement.

This gives everyone a chance to be doing something with obstacles while waiting for the tunnel. Since the ramp and teeter board are set to their introductory positions, there's little chance for accidents. But knowing NUPOs as we do, we keep a close watch on what they're doing. If anyone deviates from Three Fibs or begins to do anything that could possibly cause a setback, we immediately bring this to their attention.

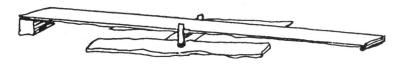

Teeter board set low and stabilized so it won't move.

Tunnel Fronts

When all the pups have been introduced to the tunnel and are comfortable with it, we use the tunnel to teach the next increment of the Front. First, we discuss what to do if the pups don't come immediately and directly to the NUPOs when called. Since this is the first time the NUPOs will call their pups while *not* holding the leash or wearing the training line, we need to explain in detail what corrective actions have to be taken if the pups do not come straight in and sit.

I explain to them, "If you call your dog, and he or she doesn't head straight to you the *first* time you call, we need to teach you to react quickly and correctly. The last thing you'll want to do is to raise your voice angrily or repeat the command. Instead, start running toward the end of the leash, praising as you go. Don't look your puppy in the eye, but concentrate on the end of the leash.

"If the pup should suddenly 'catch on' and start coming to you, just back up and keep praising until you've returned to you're starting position. If your puppy doesn't pay attention to you as you run praising toward the end of the leash, pick the leash up by the handle and give it a good jerk. Then run back to where you started, holding the leash, continuing to praise, and giving the Front hand signal all the way. Complete the Front with a Sit and reward the puppy.

Never Act Angry

"Never, ever raise your voice in anger, and remember to pick up the very *end* of the leash. If you reach for the leash near the pup's collar, the pup might back away reflexively. You must convince your puppies that you're not upset with them, so don't shout or look them in the eye. Of course, you can tell them what you really think — just make sure, 'You dumb little knucklehead, wait 'till I get my hands on the leash,' sounds sooo sweet!"

Bucket, "Front"

Over the years Nancy has worked out a demonstration of this technique that continues to crack me up. She has me hold a three gallon, plastic water bucket, that has a leash attached to the handle. My job is to toss the bucket through the tunnel when she says, "Bucket, Front!"

BUCKET, FRONT !

Obviously, this is to show NUPOs what to do if their dog stalls out on the Front, but every now and then "Bucket" somehow manages to wind up right at Nancy's feet, which of course blows the demonstration, but breaks everyone up!

The reason that Nancy doesn't use a puppy for this demonstration is that the pups have just been introduced to the tunnel, so have not yet been Fronted through it. To be called, and possibly corrected, by someone they don't know and trust in this new situation, might set up an unpleasant association between Fronting and the tunnel. Also, it's much easier to show noncompliance quickly and clearly with the bucket than a puppy!

Working With the Tunnel

We then break into Teaching Groups and line everyone up single file. We start off by putting the NUPOs about ten feet from the tunnel opening, standing up straight. They're instructed to call their pups while backing up another ten feet. We ask them to wait to call their puppies until we give the signal — otherwise they might get the instructor through the tunnel as well as the puppy! All the pups are dragging their leashes. We gradually lengthen the distance until the NUPOs are starting to call from about fifty feet while running back another fifty.

Adding Distractions

The next challenge is to add a distraction to the recall by having the team that just finished Fronting walk past the puppy coming out of the tunnel! The distance is shortened to about twenty feet so that any needed correction can be made quickly. This is continued for three repetitions for each team, and then we ask two NUPOs and their dogs to distract the dog that's running. Everyone is cautioned to be careful not to step on the dragging leashes, and, if the dogs become entangled, to drop the leashes immediately. Last, we do an out-of-sight recall from about one hundred feet with no distractions and take a water break.

Typical Problems

If everyone has kept up on the homework, the pups can readily be taught to respond while distracted. Problems usually arise when NUPOs come to class unprepared. We do our best to bring them up to speed, but if they require too much attention, we have to ask them to please take a seat and watch. We can then work with them during the break or after class.

Occasionally we'll have someone who does all the homework, but is still having problems. If the difficulty involves distance, i.e., the pup responds well when on the leash or line when distracted, but has problems responding when called from beyond ten feet, we put the pup on a twenty-five-foot training leash and ask the NUPO to do distracted Fronts off to the side while *holding* the long leash. After they can do three in a row, we try running the pup through the tunnel, but have the NUPO start off holding the long leash.

If they cannot do distracted Fronts when on the six-foot leash or ten-foot training line, we have little choice but to ask them to continue to practice at this level, and emphasize the absolute necessity of practicing with distractions. We review their teaching procedures and offer suggestions if we spot something amiss.

Fifty-Foot Light Line

After the water break, the use of the fifty-foot long line is demonstrated. Nancy picks a puppy for the demonstration, and I borrow one (or use one of our dogs) as a distraction. She removes the leash and snaps on a fifty-foot, one-eighth-inch nylon line. She doesn't hold the line, but allows the dog to *drag* it along the ground. The line must be free of knots or tangles. She starts walking from one end of the training area, and I walk toward her from the other end. By simply stepping on the line and then praising, Nancy keeps the pup within ten to fifteen feet of her. As soon as her pup becomes distracted by my dog, she calls, "Front," runs away from the pup, and, at the first sign of the slightest hesitation, picks up the line and jerks it while continuing to praise. If the puppy bolts or is very large, she steps on the line first so that it doesn't burn her hand.

Work Under Distractions

I tell them, "Most of you are at the point where your pups need to practice only when they're distracted, so hook them up to your fifty-foot light line and go looking for trouble. As soon as they give any indication that they're not going to stay with you on the walk because of distractions, call them *once*, and then jerk the line if you need to. Only do distracted Fronts three times in a row. Never allow them to get more than ten to fifteen feet away from you, or you'll run out of your safety margin of line. To keep them nearby, just step on the line and praise. And, always expect that they're not going to perform when you're working with them, so your timing will be right on!

Take Time Outs

"During the Time Outs snap on the leash and allow the pups to be distracted. Eventually you'll be able to let them drag the line and just step on it to check them if they get more than ten to fifteen away. Give them time to sniff things out and dawdle. Allow them to socialize when appropriate, but teach them to attend and respond when you call. It helps the pups be more willing to come if, after responding, they're then allowed to return to their play."

Demonstrating the Wait While Down

Next, we discuss and demonstrate the Wait while Down. Nancy again demonstrates, using several dogs of various sizes. She begins by placing the dog into a sit. Then, holding the collar and picking up both front feet, she rolls the puppy back toward her and down, using the rear as a pivot point.

Once the pup is down, she steps on the leash. Then, she signals Wait with the same command and hand signal as was used for the Wait while sitting. She positions her left hand over, but not touching, the pup's shoulders, while keeping her right, or signal, hand extended in the Wait hand signal.

Correcting While Down

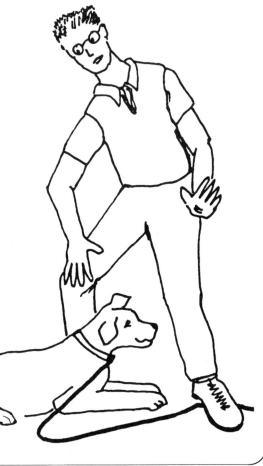

If the pup tries to get up or creep, it is corrected using a raised voice with simultaneous brisk contact with the *inside* edge of the left hand on the shoulder blade. This correction is analogous to a leash correction, but the sensation is felt from the direction that we want to discourage! If the pup rolls onto its back, but doesn't try to get up, it is *not* corrected.

I usually have to remind NUPOs to correct *only* once, then praise and take their time to reposition. I tell them, "The reason for raising your voice and making contact with your left hand is *not* to shove the pup back down. The only reason is to provide Fast Feedback for trying to leave the Down position, and, if your timing is good, the pups will quickly learn not to get up until released.

Rolling the puppy into the prone position.

"The release is the same as when you released them from the Sit/Wait. Make the "smack-smack" sound and run back about 10 feet while praising. While running back, reach into your pocket and have a food reward handy. Signal a Sit with the food hand, and complete the exercise by rewarding and praising and petting for at least five seconds."

We also have to remind them to say, "Waldo, Wait," only once, *not* to have food in their hand until after the release, and only to do three in a row.

Stability Through Distractions

Their homework on the Wait while Down is to build stability in small increments so that, by next class, they can walk completely around the pup holding the leash while about five feet away. After taking at least two days to introduce the Wait while Down, they are then asked to practice *only* when the pup is in a distracting situation.

I tell them, "Almost anyone can teach a puppy to Wait when nothing is going on and the pup is focused upon the lesson. But this isn't going to be of any value to you because when you need to use the Wait in real life situations, the pup will almost always be distracted by something. This means that if you want a reliable Wait — one that means *'Don't move from the position you're in until you're released, no matter what is going on!'* — you must practice under distracting teaching/learning conditions."

Phasing Out Food

The final piece of business is to talk to them about phasing out the food reward. I tell them, "Once the puppies have shown they can perform a command reliably under heavy distraction over a period of weeks, it's time to begin to eliminate the food reward. The reason we suggest you not make their adult performance dependent upon a food reward is that you're not always going to have food with you so, if the dog learns only to perform when you do, the commands are of little use! Even if you do manage to bring food with you, your dog may not be hungry that outing!

"This doesn't mean they shouldn't be rewarded for complying with your requests. But, as they mature and become more proficient, the rewards for working for you will come from your relationship and the work itself. All that will be needed is your enthusiastic appreciation of a job well done.

"Most of you have pups who are very reliable on the Front. What we'd like you to do is to begin phasing out the food on this command only. Do this by 'forgetting' to give it every now and then, about 25% of the time per week on a random basis. In order for this to work the pups must not be able to predict whether they'll receive a food reward and be petted and praised or just be petted and praised."

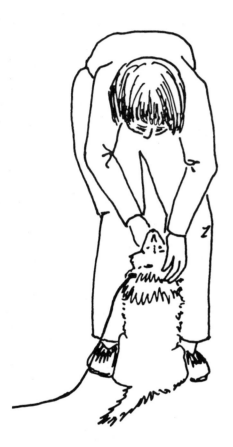

Presenting the food reward with both hands.

Present With Both Hands

Nancy demonstrates presenting and withholding food with one of the pups. She holds the food reward as usual in her right, or signal, hand and the leash in the left hand. She signals a Front, and while the pup is in the Sit, she bends down and *simultaneously* lowers both hands; one offers the food reward, the other begins to stroke the side of the pup's head and neck. After the pup takes the food, the food hand also pets. She's careful to bend down and stroke the puppy in its favorite spots and praise profusely.

Withholding Food

When the food is withheld, everything is done identically except that the food or signal hand slides past the mouth and pets. The food is still held in the signal hand, it just isn't offered. It's important to make sure that body language doesn't predict whether or not a food reward will be given. Some puppies will turn and look for the missing food, but Nancy distracts them by being especially enthusiastic with her praise and petting.

If done correctly, food withdrawal will actually increase performance. The puppies seem to work harder for the reward when it becomes less frequent. We ask them to take four to six weeks to eliminate food gradually on the recall. Food can always be used when teaching under new conditions, if there are performance decrements due to stress, when introducing new exercises, or to remotivate if performance deteriorates and the correction level must be increased.

This ends Fourth Puppy Night, but usually the NUPOs want to work with the obstacles one more time before going home. I mention that next week we'll have more obstacles for them to work with and remind them that playgrounds are loaded with interesting devices.

"Just remember Three Fibs and the safety rules, and you'll have a great time!"

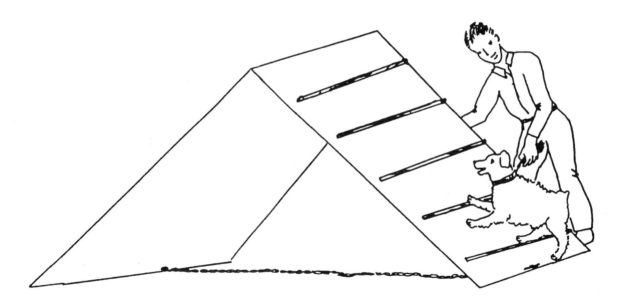

Up and over!

FIFTH PUPPY NIGHT

Teaching Fifth Puppy Night is usually very rewarding. Most NUPOs get excellent performances from their puppies, and it's exciting to see their teaching skills develop. On the other hand, the few NUPOs who are still struggling stand out like ticks on a Mexican Hairless, so we take time to give them plenty of help and encouragement.

Start by Reviewing

Class begins with a review of Controlled Walking. I ask them to "Go for a Walk," and while they're practicing, I call for "One-Handed Walking," Keep-Away," and "Quiet Walking." "Quiet Walking" means just that — don't make a sound. This begins to prepare the pup for walking down the sidewalk or into the show ring with a "normal" human being, not one who sounds like Leo Buscaglia on uppers!

Next, we ask everyone to reacquaint the pups with the obstacles they worked on last week. We suggest they start just below the level of difficulty they were last working on. If anyone missed last week's class, Nancy and I help introduce their pup to the tunnel and explain Three FIB so they can introduce the other obstacles correctly.

The goals Fifth Puppy Night are:

1. Review Three FIB.
2. Introduce the low ramp obstacle.
3. Review Sit/Waits and Down/Waits.
4. Practice Fronts and Waits under distraction using the low ramp.
5. Review phasing out food rewards on the Front.
6. Add difficulty to the V-ramp and teeter board obstacles.
7. Review the tunnel Recall.
8. Demonstrate how to teach the Drop on signal.

Introducing the Low Ramp

After the warm-up I ask for everyone to gather around and have a seat, and we talk about how they are going to introduce the new obstacle — a low ramp made from plastic milk-type crates and strapped on 2 x 12 foot boards. (See illustration on page 71.)

First I ask "Does everyone remember Three FIB? O.K., give me an I, give me an F, give me a B and a Three. F, B, I; I, F, B and Three." If the NUPOs have Three FIB memorized, they can easily keep up with the rapid fire.

I also remind them of the two big safety rules which are: only one puppy/NUPO team at a time on a obstacle, and NO HUMANS on the obstacles, ever.

I ask them to tell us how they plan to introduce the low ramp before sending them out on their own. We've found that the more we question them about how they're going to do something before they do it, the better are the pups' chances of having a good experience.

Increasing Difficulty

Before starting, we increase the level of difficulty on the V-ramp by making it steeper. The teeter board is made more difficult by removing the stabilizer. At first we have a helper hold it when the pups walk over, allowing it to move only an inch or two. We put two rigid tunnels together, making one long, L-shaped tunnel.

Obstacle Warm-Up

We divide the class into two groups, one group to introduce the low ramp, and the other group to work on the V-ramp, teeter board, and rigid tunnels. We tell them, "Go to it, and if anyone has any problems, stop and see us." Nancy and I keep track of what they're doing, and we don't hesitate to interrupt with suggestions at the first sign of problems.

Intercepting Problems

Someone may try to take a pup too far too fast. So we remind him or her *only* to do three repetitions in a row. If a pup has difficulty during a repetition, that counts as one of the three repetitions. They are reminded again to proceed *slowly* and to *please* add difficulty in *increments*.

Another relapse is luring and/or forcing the pup over or through an obstacle. If we catch someone dragging his or her pup, we put a stop to it before the poor dog decides to wait out the rest of the evening listening to dog food commercials on the car radio!

Once everyone has had plenty of time to practice, we line up all the puppy/NUPO teams single file and send them through the obstacle course one by one. This is a good way to spot any problems such as balks or refusals and to help the NUPOs improve their teaching techniques. For safety's sake we have at least two helpers at each obstacle. The helpers are those adults at class who are not working a pup.

Ramp Waits and Recalls

After three times through the course, we take a brief water break. Afterward, we again split into two groups, half working with Nancy and me on the low ramp and half working on the other obstacles.

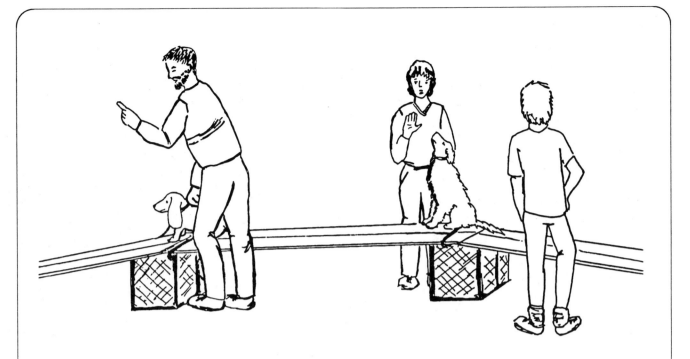

Two dogs are worked on the low ramp at the same time. One of us holds the first dog ready to do a Front while the second dog is on a Sit/Wait. If I'm holding for the Front, Nancy reviews the Waits, and vice versa. When the first puppy leaves the ramp on the Front, the second one moves up to take its place.

This is a very good way to review the NUPOs' Front and Wait teaching techniques. The other group of NUPOs and puppies working the V-ramp, tunnel, and teeter board provide excellent distractions.

On the low ramp, the pups learn to Wait under new conditions and have the added difficulty of having another pup doing a recall directly ahead of them. After everyone has a chance to do three Waits and three Fronts, we switch groups.

Double Distraction

For round two, difficulty is added by having the last two pups which completed Fronts act as distractions for the pup which is Fronting. Two NUPOs place their pups on either side of the path the Fronting pup takes when leaving the low ramp to return directly to its NUPO. Now, we have a double distraction, as the Fronting pup could cause the Waiting pups to lose their concentration and leave their Sits. After both groups have had a chance to do three repetitions using this configuration, we take another water break.

Remember to Use Both Hands

During the Front practice, we remind the NUPOs to present the food reward to their puppies with both hands as we demonstrated at the previous class. We tell them not to withhold food at this time as the ramp recalls are a new experience for the pups, and it's best to use food reinforcement when teaching something new or working under new conditions.

Hit the Deck

Nancy then demonstrates the Drop on signal. I tell them, "From a practical standpoint, dropping your dog down and asking it to Wait is more useful than the Wait while Sitting. One reason is that the pups will be able to Wait more comfortably for longer periods if they are lying down. Another reason is that it is a more stable position for them as more effort is required to leave it.

"We are going to teach you to teach your pups to Drop on signal tonight, but we are going to ask you *not* to combine it with the Wait while Down at this time. The reason is that we've found it's easier

Use forearm pressure to prompt the pup down.

for the pups to learn combined exercises if they first master each component individually. And, if you're planning to go on to competition training, it's best to guard against anticipation of commands by not linking them together during the early stages of learning."

Demonstrating the Drop

Nancy demonstrates the Drop with several pups of different sizes. She first places a pup in a Sit on her left without a command and then places her left foot, leg, or knee directly behind the pup's rear. Holding the collar with her left hand, she then places her left forearm along the pup's back and puts a food reward in her right hand. (Sometimes small breed puppies can best be taught by placing them directly in front of the handler between the knees.)

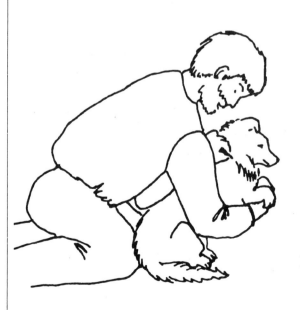

Scooping out the front legs.

She starts with her food (or signal) hand just above the pup's head with the palm down and turned away from the dog. Then she says, "Waldo, Drop," and simultaneously moves her signal hand out and down to the ground while putting downward pressure on the pup's back with the left forearm. Praise follows the command immediately and, as in the Recall, continues through presentation of the food reward and petting. When the pup is *all* the way down, she immediately turns her hand over and offers the food. The signal should be given so that the food hand winds up well in front of the pup, so he's inclined to stretch forward to reach the reward.

Most pups will simply follow the signal hand down with little resistance. Some, however, will resist. We found that either gently scooping out the front feet with the signal hand, or starting with the front feet placed well forward (off balance) will get around most resistances.

We have to remind the NUPOs to make sure they praise *immediately* after giving the Drop Signal. Another important part of this teaching method is to make sure they keep the pup's rear trapped against their foot, leg, or knee.

If the rear isn't kept on the ground while prompting the Drop, they lose the pivot point, and wind up trying to shove the dog down with their hand on the neck scruff, while the pup is standing up! This naturally leads to increased resistance on the dog's part and is unacceptable.

Subordination Helps the Drop

We've found that those NUPOs who have worked successfully on the subordination exercises seem to have little trouble with the Drop. A couple of things are probably involved. First, they have established a leadership relationship with the dog so there's less resistance, and second, the dog is accustomed to lying down for them so there's less apprehension.

Withdrawing the Food Reward

Before handing out the homework and sending them home, we review phasing out the food reward on the recall. They should begin in earnest this week by "forgetting" to give the food reward about 25% of the time on a random basis. The dog should never be able to figure out exactly which time it will receive a food reward.

Over the next four weeks of working with their puppies, the food is *gradually* leaned out at the rate of about 25% per week as they continue to teach in a variety of locations under heavy distraction.

When they teach in a new location, they should bring the density of food reinforcement up to about 100%. And, food is always used on a 100% basis when introducing *new* exercises or in particularly *stressful* learning situations.

Forecast Graduation

This concludes Fifth Puppy Night, but before they leave, we remind them that next week will be their graduation and talk about the importance of doing their homework. They are to continue to teach the recall on the fifty-foot line and Controlled Walking in distracting, difficult situations. They should also be able to have their pups do a Sit/Wait on the fifty-foot line from fifteen feet away in distracting situations.

We also forecast that graduation will consist of teaching the pups to run an obstacle course using those obstacles they have worked with as well as brand new obstacles. We make sure that they understand that the graduation is a no pressure, noncompetitive, teaching class. The idea is to challenge in a realistic and meaningful way the NUPO's ability to teach and to give the pups further opportunity to work with one of their favorite things at class — the puppy obstacles!

SIXTH PUPPY NIGHT — GRADUATION

S uperPuppy Class graduation is a teaching class, not a pass-or-fail test for the NUPOs and their puppies. We feel that all too much emphasis is placed upon competitiveness when teaching dog training classes. In our class, we have tried to de-emphasize competition and emphasize building a relationship based upon trust, respect, affection, and communication — a relationship from which *all* future performance can be derived.

A Non-Competitive Graduation

A competitive, judged, and scored graduation, especially in a puppy or entry-level class, can place the dog in a no-win situation. If it does well, the handler receives most of the praise, but if things go poorly, the dog is usually blamed.

However, if competition training is viewed as a means by which the dog can continue to grow and develop to its full potential as an integral part of family life, it can provide both dog and handler with many benefits. Unfortunately, it has been our experience that all too many exhibitors and fanciers use competition as a means to satisfy certain human, ego-related desires. As a result, they sacrifice their relationships with one of the most remarkable animals on earth for political, emotional, and/or monetary considerations.

Therefore, we feel the primary role of all introductory level classes should be to teach relationship-building, not competition training. For without a close positive relationship built upon *mutual* trust, respect, and affection, the chances of a NUPO keeping his or her dog through adulthood, much less becoming a contributing member of the dog fancy, are not very good at all.

Our experience has been that a competitive-style graduation can put too much pressure on NUPOs who are just beginning to establish a relationship with their puppies; who may still be struggling for understanding; or who just may not feel comfortable having to perform in front of a group. We found that if we provide them with a relatively pressure-free, fun-but-challenging experience at their last class, they'll learn more and not leave with feelings of inferiority about themselves and/or their puppies — and, of course, the *dogs* will have a better time of it.

The Graduation Obstacle Course

When the NUPOs arrive at graduation, we have the following obstacles already set up:
1. Two tunnels.
2. One inclined jump.

3. One twelve-foot extension ladder with its two sections separated and lying on the ground.
4. Teeter board with stabilizer available for those who need it.
5. V-ramp.
6. V-barrier.
7. Weave poles.
8. Low ramp.

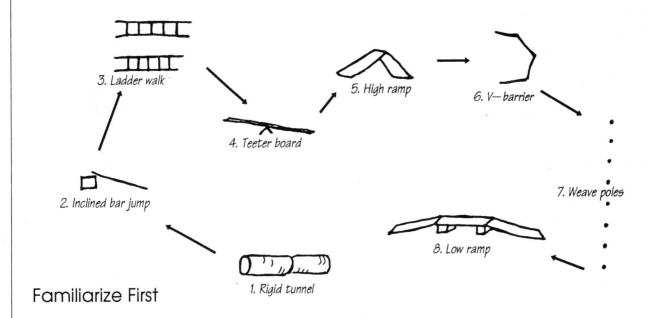

3. Ladder walk

5. High ramp

6. V—barrier

4. Teeter board

2. Inclined bar jump

7. Weave poles

8. Low ramp

1. Rigid tunnel

Familiarize First

The first task for the NUPOs is to familiarize the pups with the new obstacles by allowing them to walk around and investigate them. We ask them not to do any training, just acquaint the pups with the new obstacles and reacquaint them with the ones they've already used.

We also ask them to warm up the pups by practicing their Controlled Walking, Fronts, and Waits independently of the obstacles.

Explaining the Course

After everyone is warmed up, I ask them to take a seat and Nancy demonstrates with one of our dogs exactly what their teaching goals are for tonight.

I then tell them, "The idea is for you to teach your pups to negotiate the obstacle course in a particular fashion when holding the leash or with the leash dragging. The first obstacle is the tunnel. The goal for this obstacle is to Drop your puppy and have it Wait at the tunnel entrance while you drop the leash and walk away about thirty feet. Then call your pup, using Front, to complete the exercise.

"Next comes the inclined jump. Because you can vary the height at which you ask your pup to take the jump, pups of any size can safely use it. Please don't jump the bar yourself as you may trip and startle your pup or injure yourself! Hold the leash so that it doesn't interfere with your puppy's movement when it jumps.

"After the jump is the teeter board. Your goal tonight is to teach them to walk across it without the stabilizer. After walking the teeter board, proceed to the V-ramp. Notice that it's at a steeper angle tonight, so be sure to hold your pups by their collars the first few times you attempt it.

"This obstacle is followed by the ladder walk. The goal here is to teach them to walk over the ladder rungs the long way. Next, go to the V-barrier and teach them to Wait while sitting inside the "V", then drop the leash and move about thirty feet away on the other side of the barrier and do a Front.

"Finally, we have the weave poles and the low ramp. Teach them to walk in and out of the weave poles on leash with you without pulling on the leash or tangling you in the poles! Finally, teach your puppy to Wait either sitting or lying down on the low ramp. Drop the leash, go about thirty feet away, and then call with a Front."

How To Teach The Course

We then discuss how best to teach the exercises using the Three FIB technique. Since this is a graduation class, we want to encourage the NUPOs to think on their own, so we try not to "spoon feed" them with recipe-type instructions on how to go about working with each

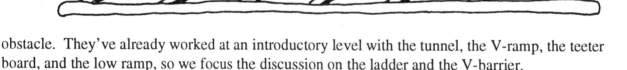

obstacle. They've already worked at an introductory level with the tunnel, the V-ramp, the teeter board, and the low ramp, so we focus the discussion on the ladder and the V-barrier.

Usually the class will have no trouble devising a procedure using Three FIB to teach the ladder obstacle by placing the pup very close to the "back" or "exit" end of a ladder and guiding it out with praise and a reward. They will then use increments and Fast Feedback to accomplish the entire task.

The V-barrier presents a more complex teaching task as not only do the NUPOs have to teach a brief out of sight Wait, but must teach their pups first to move away from the sound of their "Front" and go around the barrier in order to get to them! We prompt them to figure out that it will work well to start with the puppy Waiting very close to the open end of the "V." The increments consist of gradually moving the puppy back toward the apex or center of the obstacle. The first increments are done on leash with very short

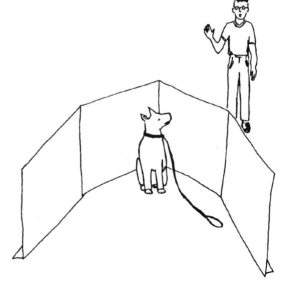

Fronts. Later the leash is dropped so that they can move further away.

I tell them to take their time and think through each teaching procedure before diving in. We want them to remember to have fun as this isn't a test, and it's really *for the pups*. We emphasize the importance of not getting egos involved by thinking in terms of a competitive performance. They should take plenty of Time Outs, and come over and talk to us if they run into problems.

Evaluate During The Practice Period

It usually takes a class of sixteen about thirty minutes to finish teaching the course. Unknown to the NUPOs , Nancy and I evaluate their performances during the practice session. We do this because, over the years, we've found that our best indications of how they are going to work with their pups at home occur when they are working anonymously within the group and not "performing" individually.

While the NUPOs are practicing, we interfere only if someone is teaching in such a way that the pup is in danger of having a bad experience or if they ask for help.

Optional Individual Run-Throughs

We take a water break when we feel everyone has had ample time to prepare. After the break, we have optional, individual run-throughs. I tell them, "When I call your name, just say, 'pass,' if for any reason you do not want to run through. Don't worry, you'll still graduate. If you're having trouble teaching the Waits tonight, but still want to try the course, one of us will be glad to hold your pup for you. Tonight is not the night to try to make them do anything you haven't prepared them for."

Oddly enough, almost all the NUPOs run through individually to the applause and cheers of the other class members. During the run-throughs, I take time to comment to the class as a whole on what they're watching. Pointing out what a particular NUPO is doing that is effective and what he or she could improve upon helps the class members focus on the elements of good teaching.

Graduation and Beyond

Finally, the NUPOs receive a graduation certificate, and the pups receive a SuperPuppy® bandanna! We also have homework describing how to completely phase out food and the fifty-foot training line on the Front and how to progress on the Wait and the Drop commands.

Someone usually asks about further levels of training. We describe the Advanced SuperPuppy Classes and use one of our dogs to show them some of the things that are covered.

After a spay/neuter pep talk, we answer any other questions and tell them that, although they have laid down a terrific foundation for the future, they have just barely tapped their pups' tremendous potentials. As the dogs grow and mature, they will be able to do amazing things together if they KEEP WORKING!

Saying "Good-bye"

I tell them, "Because you are teaching your pups that performing particular tasks for you is fun and rewarding as it involves learning and doing new things, meeting new individuals, and going to different places, you can soon think about providing a way for them to express their instinctive abilities under controlled conditions. Not only will this strengthen your relationship beyond belief, but your dogs will be doing something all too few family dogs in this country are given the opportunity to do — WORK!"

I then mention some of the many avenues open to them such as agility, herding, hunting, carting, coaching, coursing, sledding, search and rescue, scent hurdles, road trials, field trials, tracking, guarding, going to ground, flyball, Frisbee®, conformation, and obedience!

What Nancy and I have tried to do in SuperPuppy Class is show them the why, what, and how. Now it's up to them to complete the process so they can truly wind up with a great pet, the best dog they'll ever have!

As far as the notorious Waldo is concerned, he seems to be quite a different beast. In the space of only seven weeks, he's changed from an accident waiting to happen into a young canine that is able to listen to his elders and not *always* act impulsively, and he's learned to overcome physical, mental, and emotional challenges.

What's really amazing is that he acts as if he is really enjoying his new role in life as a subordinate member of his adopted human pack. I don't know if the wolves on Ellesmere Island would be proud of him or not, but Nancy and I sure are!

<u>NOTES</u>

NOTES

HOMEWORK HANDOUTS

ORIENTATION HANDOUT

TO REMEMBER FOR THE FIRST CLASS NIGHT

1. REQUIRED: An up-to-date INOCULATION RECORD from your veterinarian. We need to know the dates and types of all immunizations your puppy has received. We require DHLP-PARVO-CORONA and BORDETELLA. There are NO exceptions.
2. RECOMMENDED: Results of a fecal exam for internal parasites within 3 weeks of the start of class.
3. Buckle or Snap-Lock collar — plain, good quality leather or nylon.
4. 6 ft. leash — good quality, flat leather, nylon, or canvas, not chain or rope. Should be separate from the collar and have a loop handle.
5. Food treats for your puppy that are very small or can easily be broken up.
6. A nonbreakable water dish for your puppy.
7. Please wear comfortable clothing and low-heeled, soft-soled shoes.
8. And, of course . . . *your puppy!* Please don't feed him after 12 noon on each class day.

READ THE *SUPERPUPPY* BOOK! WE WILL BE REFERRING TO IT OFTEN!

The Leash and Collar

The leash and collar are two of your most important pieces of training equipment. Good quality equipment will last a long time and be effective in helping you teach your dog. Poor quality, inappropriate, or ill-fitting equipment can hinder your teaching and be potentially dangerous should it break or come loose. Pay special attention to the bolt snap and other hardware.

Your puppy's collar must fit well. For training, only *one* finger width should fit easily between the collar and the puppy's neck. For your puppy's safety, the collar shouldn't be left on while he's unsupervised.

If your puppy hasn't worn a collar yet, he may need time to get used to having something around his neck. We've found it helps if the collar is first put on shortly before a meal and removed soon after. Don't leave it on too long, and every time it's put on, offer the puppy a small food treat. Most puppies will quickly accept wearing a collar if it's introduced in this way.

For teaching purposes, the leash must be six feet long — no longer and no shorter!! And no wider than approximately 5/8 inch. People with small breeds should use a narrower leash. If you have a leash at home, *please* check it before bringing it to class. The bolt snap should be in proportion to the size of the dog. Flat nylon, canvas, or leather leashes are required for class because training with a chain or rope type leash is difficult, if not impossible.

Read and begin working on the assignment on Exercise, page 34 in your *SuperPuppy* book.

Preparing to Come to Class

Your goals for next week are to have your puppy accustomed to walking with you while on the leash and collar and to take your puppy to a new place each day.

Some puppies will fight or fear the leash when first learning to walk with it on. In order to develop a happy attitude toward walking on leash with you, we recommend that you take the following steps.

1. Put the leash and collar on the pup in the house and let him move about dragging the leash. Use food, petting, play, and Happy Talk to make the puppy's experience a pleasant one.

2. Once the puppy is moving freely, pick up the loop at the end of the leash and move with the puppy. Do not restrain him, and don't pull or jerk on the leash. It is important that the puppy move eagerly and eventually begin to pull you of his own accord.

3. When the puppy is pulling you through the house, it's time to go outside and repeat step #2. Take your puppy in the car to a new location each day before class starts, and meet three new people at each location using the procedure demonstrated at Orientation.

If your puppy is already used to a leash and collar and moves eagerly when you go for a walk, skip steps #1 and #2, but *take your puppy to a new location every day and have him meet three new people each time.*

"Chew-Proofing" Your Leash

If your puppy is inclined to chew his leash, you may want to "chew-proof" it. We find that most people are successful using a product called Bitter Apple®, which is available in pet stores. This procedure is explained in the *SuperPuppy* book, and will also work to help teach your pup not to chew other items — except hands and arms!

As Bitter Apple® is alcohol-based, you must re-spray the leash daily until the lesson is learned. Menthol-based ointments such as Vick's® or Mentholatum® can be used as longer lasting alternatives.

(Instructors may also want to include a list of "ground rules" which apply to their classes.)

CLASS I — The First Night With Puppies

1. CONTROLLED WALKING: One lesson that your puppy needs to learn as it starts to become "civilized" is to walk easily on a loose leash. Dogs who haven't learned this lesson often take their owners for a walk instead of the other way around!

YOUR PUPPY MUST BE ACTIVELY PULLING ON THE LEASH TO LEARN THIS LESSON. If he's not pulling, or if we have instructed you to do so, first use the Alternative Method described later. DO NOT USE THE FOLLOWING LEASH JERK METHOD IF YOUR PUPPY "STALLS OUT," BALKS, or LAGS BEHIND.

The first step in teaching Controlled Walking is to teach the pup not to pull on the leash.

With the six-foot leash and buckle collar on your pup, begin by holding the loop of the leash in *both* hands. Your hands should be close together, palms down, waist high, and slightly out from your body. Your elbows should be slightly flexed, and you should feel comfortable and strong! The leash must be at its full length; *do not* gather it up.

Size of loop exaggerated for clarity.

Start to teach by giving the verbal signal — "(Puppy's name), let's go for a walk!" Your tone of voice should be clear, distinct, and happy. If your puppy lunges ahead or to the side, jerk sharply on the leash. To be effective, the jerk must occur *just before* the leash becomes tight. *Don't raise your voice or make any verbal correction.* Use continuous, enthusiastic Happy Talk. The leash provides the Teaching Action by feeding back to the puppy that he has made a wrong choice. Your voice provides encouragement and reassurance. Your puppy's tail should be up and wagging, and he should be paying attention.

After walking eight to ten steps, give your pup the Time Out signal, a smacking, kissing sound, and drop down on one knee. Offer a treat to emphasize the "smack-smack" sound. Then allow your pup a Time Out to play, sniff, or "do his own thing." Your puppy is allowed to pull at this time.

You can teach the Controlled Walking exercise frequently during the week, but remember that your teaching segments should be very short and the Time Out should be relatively long. As you become comfortable with the technique and your pup gets the idea of walking *with you* on a loose leash, increase the distance you ask the pup to walk before taking a Time Out. By next week, the teaching segments should be approximately one minute long and no more than a total of 10 - 15% of any walk, no matter how long the walk.

If at any time your puppy begins to balk, lag behind, or act reluctant to walk with you, discontinue this method and use the Alternative Method.

Alternative Walking Method

In order for your teaching relationship with your dog to be a happy one, it's important for him to like his leash. Very young, timid, or sensitive pups or pups who have no experience with the leash should be introduced to it gradually.

Please refer to the Orientation handout and review the section, "Preparing to Come to Class." Do not progress further until you and your puppy have mastered the skills described in that section. DO NOT jerk or tug on the leash until your puppy is completely relaxed and is actively *pulling* whenever you go for a walk. NEVER, under any circumstances, pull or drag your puppy against his will. If he does not want to move on his own, simply pick him up and carry him or drop down and use Happy Talk and the "smack-smack" sound to encourage him toward you.

Once he's actively pulling on the leash, you can begin to encourage him to walk with you. Holding the leash as instructed in the "Controlled Walking" section, kneel down and coax your puppy to come to you, using the "smack-smack" sound and a happy, enthusiastic voice. As soon as he arrives, reward him with a treat, more praise, and plenty of petting. If at any time during your teaching sessions he shows signs of fearful reluctance, immediately drop down to his level and use Happy Talk and the "smack-smack" sound to encourage him to move toward you. Give him a food reward when he arrives. DO NOT JERK THE LEASH!

As your puppy learns to follow you, gradually increase the distance that you ask him to travel before being rewarded.

It is imperative that all teaching sessions be lighthearted, happy, and brief. Don't be serious or stern in your teaching, or you may destroy your puppy's enjoyment of working with you and adversely affect your relationship in general.

Once the pup has overcome his timidity and/or reluctance, you may use the regular Controlled Walking procedure. Be very careful with the intensity of your leash jerk as over-correction can cause him to stop trusting you. Sensitive or submissive dogs should be trained with a light hand on the leash and plenty of praise. If at any time your puppy becomes momentarily reluctant or fearful, revert to the Alternative Method until his attitude is confident and willing.

2. SUBORDINATION: Subordination is a natural process which results in the establishment of a relationship between you and your dog based on trust and respect. If your dog learns at an early age that you can handle his body in a pleasant, yet confident way, the chances that he will grow up to respect you will be greatly increased. Grooming and other physical care will also be much easier to accomplish.

Do the exercises as practiced in class *at least* five times a day. Your goal is to have confidence that you can do these exercises any time and anywhere with your puppy. Teach other family members to do these exercises, but we recommend that children *only* do them under your supervision. A detailed explanation of the exercises can be found in the *SuperPuppy* book.

Please call and talk with one of us if you or another family member has persistent difficulty practicing these handling exercises, if your puppy becomes more unruly during your subordination sessions this week, or if your puppy shows any signs of guarding food, toys, or other objects from you or other family members.

3. NEW EXPERIENCES: It is extremely important to begin exposing your puppy to a variety of new experiences while he is still young. In order to be a super companion and friend, he will need to be relaxed and confident in public. Older dogs who have led sheltered lives often become frightened or unmanageable when confronted by street noises, crowds of people, stairs, car riding, strangers, or other unfamiliar experiences.

To guard against this happening to you and your puppy, we suggest the following: 1) Practice your lessons at a new location *every day*. Try shopping centers, parks permitting dogs, streets, friends' homes, etc. Try to give your puppy as many *varied* experiences as you can. 2) Take your puppy with you on routine errands as much as is feasible. Show him off! 3) If your puppy has difficulty overcoming any hesitancy, go to quiet places at first. Gradually work up to busier areas. Use lots of Happy Talk and food rewards. Don't baby or try to protect your puppy. Be jolly and confident so that he will feel more carefree and outgoing. 4) If your puppy barks or growls at other people or animals in an inappropriate situation, raise your voice and jerk the leash firmly. Reward with praise when he responds. If you continue to have trouble, please talk with one of us for specific techniques to work with shyness or aggression.

REMEMBER: Dogs and *especially* puppies overheat easily so leaving your dog in the car, even with the windows cracked, can be *very dangerous*. Even on a cloudy day, a car left in the open can rapidly turn into an oven.

NEXT WEEK: In addition to your regular equipment, please bring your puppy's brush.

CLASS II — Beginning a Reliable Recall

1. TEACHING THE RECALL: Because we feel that the most important *skill* your puppy can learn at class is to come *reliably* when called, we strongly suggest that you do this assignment at least twice every day.

When your dog is first learning to come, he'll learn faster if you make it very pleasant for him to approach you. So, *never* call your puppy to you and make him do something he doesn't like, and *never, ever* call him to you for discipline. Coming to you should mean praise, treats, petting, play, or other things that he enjoys.

Remember, at this age, his attention span for training is short. Your teaching sessions will be more effective and enjoyable for both of you if you have a happy, fun attitude and take frequent Time Outs and *only do three repetitions in a row.*

INTRODUCTION TO THE RECALL — PHASE I, COMING AND SITTING: 1) Hold the six-foot leash *by the loop* in *one hand only.* If you're right-handed, use your right hand on the

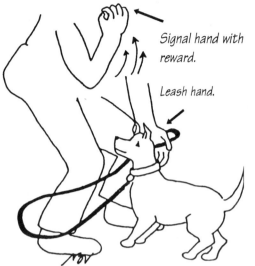

Signal hand with reward.

Leash hand.

leash. Several small pieces of food are held in the other hand. 2) Start by letting the pup take *you* for a walk. Do not use the Controlled Walking command at this time. 3) Make the "smack-smack" sound and quickly back away from your puppy about eight feet, encouraging him to come using continuous, super-enthusiastic Happy Talk. Simultaneously, move your free (food) hand repeatedly toward your chest as a hand signal for the puppy to come. If necessary, *jerk* the leash to focus your pup's attention on you. 4) When your pup is close to you, show him the Sit signal, and, if necessary, shape him into a Sit.

SHAPING THE SIT: Hook a finger of the hand holding the leash into his collar and gently lift up. If necessary, *tuck* his rear under with the other hand .

Continue praising while shaping the Sit. DO NOT FORCE THE SIT BY PUSHING DOWN ON HIS BACK. It's very important that this part of the lesson be done *patiently* and *gently* so that your puppy is eager to come to you and Sit. NO VERBAL COMMAND FOR THE SIT IS GIVEN.

5) Once your pup is *securely* seated, show him the Sit signal once more, then reward with the food treat. Pet and praise your puppy lavishly for 5 seconds. Continue to praise throughout the exercise. 6) As he learns to Sit automatically, hesitate for a few seconds before offering the food reward. Do Phase I three times in a row. Take a Time Out. Repeat.

PHASE II, THE VERBAL COMMAND: Once you and your puppy are proficient at the above procedure (usually two to three days), introduce the verbal Recall command. 1) Begin as in PHASE I, but call your puppy, saying, "(Puppy's name), 'smack-smack,' Front!" Praise follows *immediately* and *continuously.* The "smack-smack" may be dropped out after the first set of three. 2) ONLY SAY THE COMMAND ONCE. Use the Teaching Action of the leash jerk to get your puppy's attention if he's distracted. 3) Complete the Sit and reward as above. Do three in a row. Take a break. Repeat.

From now on only call your pup using the hand signal and Front command when he's *on the training equipment.* Once your pup is responding well, take him to *new places* to practice the Recall and Controlled Walking. Your puppy must perform under distraction in order to master the Recall.

2. CONTINUING CONTROLLED WALKING: By now your pup should be paying attention to your whereabouts during the teaching segments of your walks. "Keep-Away" is a game you can play to focus attention on you and to make the lessons more fun. 1) As before, hold the leash loop

in both hands and give the Controlled Walking command, "(Puppy's name), let's go for a walk!" 2) With *lots* of enthusiastic Happy Talk, attempt to get away from your dog by making quick changes of speed or direction. 3) If your pup doesn't pay attention, jerk the leash while praising. 4) After a brief teaching segment (approximately 10 changes), make the "smack-smack" sound, drop down, and reward. Score the game — one point for your pup when he sticks with you during a change; one point for you if you have to jerk the leash. If *you* consistently win or tie, review the basic walking technique to improve your pup's skill level.

3. INTRODUCING GROOMING: The subordinate position is an ideal place to introduce your puppy to grooming. Brushing should be introduced slowly and gently so that the sensations are pleasant.

Place the pup in the subordinate position. Keep your strong hand on the neck scruff to correct any struggling. Start out *very gently* using the back of the brush. Then gradually introduce the bristle side of the brush until, by the end of the week, you are giving a thorough brushing. Continue to handle feet, ears, mouth, etc. to prepare for nail clipping, ear cleaning, and other care-taking procedures.

As your puppy becomes accustomed to the sensations, you can introduce the pin brush, slicker brush or comb that you may also want to use for grooming. The way in which you teach him to accept being groomed will probably determine his lifelong attitude toward it, so take care when performing procedures that may cause discomfort. During grooming you may want to give your pup treats along with lots of praise and petting. Be sure that early grooming sessions are very short.

4. INTRODUCING THE BATH: Because dog bathing may be a new experience for both you and your pup, we suggest that you introduce it *like all new experiences,* gradually and gently, so that the sensations won't be overwhelming.

Begin by *briefly* putting the pup into an empty sink or tub and rewarding with praise, petting, and a treat. Repeat several times. A little later, return him to the tub and run the water, but without getting him wet. Praise, pet, and offer a treat. Once this produces no apprehension, put a small amount of water in the tub and allow him to "get his feet wet." Continue with encouragement and treats. If this experience is especially difficult, go *slowly* and use a "high power" treat such as meat or cheese. As your puppy relaxes, continue to get him used to the water by gently wetting his body with your hands, a sponge, or wash cloth.

NEXT WEEK: Bring swabs, cotton balls, alcohol, witch hazel or other astringent, baby oil, and DOG nail clippers. We will be working on nail clipping and ear cleaning and discussing other care-taking procedures.

CLASS III — Continuing the Recall & Learning to Stay Put

1. RECALL TRAINING, PART II — THE LIGHT LINE RECALL: Because it will help take you a step closer to the goal of having your dog come off-leash, you'll begin using a nylon training line this week. Using a fifty-foot line in the weeks to come, you'll practice Recalls from a distance. The lines are very light and strong, and is less obvious to the puppy than his leash.

Start out by practicing this lesson in and around your home, but then take your puppy to new locations throughout the rest of the week. Your puppy should learn to come *no matter where he is* — *not* just in your home or yard. We recommend that *whenever* you take your puppy out, you attach a light line to his collar and use the opportunity to teach him to respond to your commands. In order to learn to come reliably, your puppy *must* be taught in a variety of distracting situations and *never* be given the opportunity to ignore your call without being corrected.

1) Tie your six-foot leash around your waist. Fasten the light line to your waist by putting the looped end around the leash, passing the end with the bolt snap through the loop and cinching it up. Then attach the bolt snap to your pup's collar. 2) While walking with your pup, *wait until he becomes distracted.* Then change direction and simultaneously call, using your hand signal and verbal "Front." The signals are followed *immediately* by Happy Talk. By moving away from your puppy as you call, you will automatically jerk the line if necessary. 3) If you need to, shape the sit with the left hand. The right (signal) hand then offers the treat. Remember to stand up straight. The signal hand should be at your chest until the puppy is in a stable sit; then praise and pet for a *minimum* of five seconds. 4) REMEMBER: The verbal command is only given *once;* then Happy Talk is used throughout the puppy's return and sit. Keep the line free from knots and check it periodically for signs of wear.

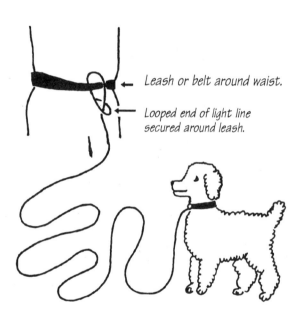

Leash or belt around waist.

Looped end of light line secured around leash.

2. TEACHING THE SIT-WAIT: It's very useful for your dog to learn to stay where he's put until released. The Wait command can be used to insure that your pup is quiet and well-behaved when necessary or stays away from potential hazards. Most dogs learn a reliable Wait if any change of position is *immediately* corrected and staying in position is rewarded. At first the Wait should be kept brief, then gradually lengthened over a period of days. In order to learn this lesson without becoming confused, your puppy must learn to remain in the position in which the command is given. Waits *must* be taught under distraction once the lesson has been introduced.

Jerk the leash upward to correct.

INTRODUCTION TO THE SIT/WAIT: 1) Attach the six-foot leash to your pup's collar. 2) With the puppy at your side and the leash in one hand, shape him into a Sit by tucking his rear under with your free hand. No command or signal is given at this time. 3) Extend the open palm of your free hand toward the pup's nose and simultaneously command, "(Puppy's name), Wait." Keep your eyes on the pup and be prepared to feed back *instantly* any attempt to move away or lie down with a brisk, upward jerk on the leash and a raised voice. Then praise your puppy and take your time to replace him *gently* into the sit. Show the hand signal *without* the verbal command. Remember that during the Wait the leash *must* remain loose, except when you are correcting. 4) Keep your hand extended in the Wait signal as a reminder to stay. The pup doesn't have to look at it 100% of the time, and he can move his head, shift his weight, or make other minor movements, just so long as he does not attempt to leave the Sit position. 5) If your pup does try to move from the Sit, quickly make the correction, then gently reposition him in the Sit with quiet praise. Show the hand signal without the verbal command. 6) Release after three to ten seconds of non-movement by making the "smack-smack" sound and moving away *at least* ten feet. This makes it *very clear* that it's now all right for your pup to move. Reward with praise, petting, and a treat. Gradually increase the time that your puppy Waits, so that by next class, he can Wait for one minute. 7) Gradually begin to move away from him until he will remain Waiting when you are at the end of the six-foot leash. 8) Also, gradually begin to move from side to side until you can walk all the way around your pup while he Waits. Don't forget to practice in different locations and under distraction.

2. CONTINUING CONTROLLED WALKING: By now you and your puppy should be skilled at walking together. If you are still having problems, please see one of us for some extra hints.

This week begin "One-handed Walking": 1) Hold the leash in your strong hand only, and gather it up to about four feet.. Use your other hand as a signal to the dog by patting your leg when starting out and changing speed or direction. 2) Also practice the Silent Walking (no praise) with the leash at six feet, and REMEMBER, if your dog attempts to pull, jerk the leash *just before* it becomes tight. This will begin to teach your pup *never* to pull you around — even on Time Outs!

Basic Puppy Care

Regular grooming and care-taking are necessary to your puppy's well-being. Use the subordination techniques to teach your puppy to be quiet and relaxed while you work on him.

FOOT CARE: Short nails make it easier for your puppy to walk and ensure good foot development. Most dogs find nail clipping somewhat less than pleasant, and a careful introduction should make things easier for both of you.

Equipment: Nail clippers, Quik-Stop® or other styptic powder or a bar of soap, scissors if your dog has a long coat, treats.

1) Start with your pup on its side. 2) Begin handling the toes and nails while making sure that your pup remains quiet. 3) Holding one paw firmly, press down on one pad so that the nail extends, and cut off just a *tiny bit* of the hook of the nail tip. Praise and offer a treat. Only do *one* more nail at this sitting. 4) No matter how careful you are, you may accidentally cut too close and cause the nail to bleed. Simply dip the nail into the styptic powder or scrape it along the surface of a soft bar of soap. Keep the puppy quiet for a few minutes to allow a clot to form. 5) Until you and your puppy are comfortable and relaxed with nail clipping, only do two or three nails at a time. 6) Some

long-haired breeds may also need to have the excess hair on their feet trimmed from around the pads. This will contribute to the development of sound feet and make it more difficult for burrs to become embedded. 7) Some dogs have "dewclaws" on the inside of their front and/or back legs.

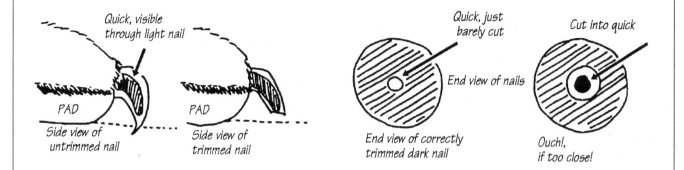

Special care should be take to keep these nails short, as injury can result if they are allowed to get too long.

EAR CARE: From time to time, most dogs' ears need to be cleaned, but breeds with hanging, heavily-furred ears usually need the most attention.

Equipment: Rubbing alcohol or other astringent, baby oil, high quality cotton swabs, cotton balls, scissors, treats.

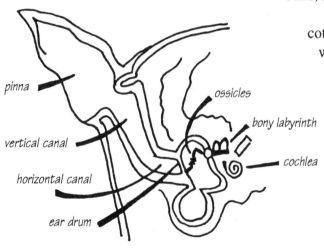

THE CANINE EAR

1) With your puppy on its side, moisten a cotton ball *lightly* with the astringent and gently wipe the inner surfaces of the ear to remove dirt, excess wax, and debris. Use the swab to clean the folds and crevices. 2) Once all exterior dirt is removed, gently insert a swab into the upper ear canal. 3) Apply a drop or two of baby oil to a finger and rub it well the ear tissue to help prevent irritation. 4) Reward good behavior with praise and a treat. 5) Hair growing inside the ear may need to be removed in order to prevent ear problems from developing. Use the scissors to trim it short or follow your veterinarian's or breeder's instructions.

Some signs that may indicate ear problems: excessive head shaking or rubbing and pawing at ears, scratching, a bad odor around ears, redness or sensitivity, discharge. Consult your veterinarian for treatment. Remember that a clean, dry ear usually stays healthy.

DENTAL HYGIENE: Your puppy should learn to allow you to examine his mouth and care for his teeth. Although dogs have little problem with tooth decay, gum disease is one of the most common problems seen by veterinarians. This can cause inflammation, bad breath, loose and infected teeth, and eventual loss of teeth. In severe cases periodontal disease can lead to serious generalized infections. Feeding dry dog food and providing appropriate chewing items are helpful, but are usually not enough.

Equipment: Soft toothbrush or cloth, commercial DOG toothpaste or other dental care products.

1) Begin with your puppy on his side. Accustom him to having his mouth and teeth handled. 2) Once he's relaxed, apply cleaner to your brush or cloth and gently massage the outside of one or two teeth. 3) Once he accepts having the outer surfaces of his teeth cleaned, open his mouth wide and gradually teach him to accept cleaning of the inner surfaces of the teeth. *Ideally* teeth should be cleaned once a week. Some signs that mean you may need to consult your veterinarian: inflamed gum-line, tartar formation, persistent foul mouth odor, bleeding, receded or eroded gums, loose teeth, missing teeth, infected teeth. If your dog breaks a tooth, contact your veterinarian for advice.

Examining your dog's mouth should be a regular part of your care-taking activities. Check the lips for inflammation, especially if you have a dog with pendulous lips or hanging flews.

Your puppy will begin to acquire his permanent teeth at four to five months of age. During this period, his mouth may be sore and gums swollen. He may be briefly "off his feed." You may

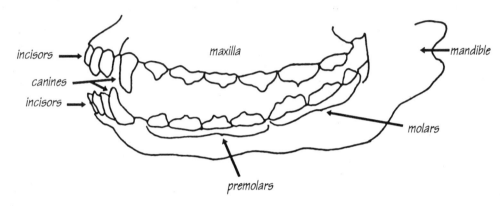

want to feed softened food if your pup seems especially sensitive. Also check frequently to make sure that baby teeth are not being retained and that your puppy's bite is normal for his breed or type.

CLASS IV — Learning to Stay Put, Part II

1. THE WAIT WHILE DOWN: 1) Place your puppy down, and put your foot on the leash. 2) With your left hand poised over the puppy's shoulders, give the command, "(Puppy's name), Wait," and hand signal as you did for the Sit/Wait. 3) If your puppy attempts to move out of the down position or creep forward, be prepared to correct by raising your voice and using the *inner edge* of your LEFT HAND in a *brief* downward chop against the shoulders. This is fast feedback only, *not* a shove or an attempt to reposition the dog. 4) Then *gently* place the pup back in the down position while quietly praising. 5) Gradually progress by increasing the distance and time as you did in the Sit/Wait. Keep in mind that it is essential for reliable performance to work in different locations under distraction. Remember: Never do more than three in a row.

Place your foot on the leash.

2. CONTINUING THE SIT/WAIT: Continue to work on the Sit/Wait, but not at the same time as the Wait While Down. If you are progressing well: 1) Give the command, "(Puppy's name), Sit," before giving the Wait command and signal. The hand signal for the Sit is an upward motion of your right arm to your chest — just as at the end of the recall! Remember to praise immediately after the command and to shape the Sit if he doesn't respond right away. At first a food reward is appropriate. Then, on a random basis, either release your pup or give the Wait command and signal. Sometimes do the Wait after placing the puppy in the Sit. 2) When the pup is steady under distraction at the end of the six-foot leash, attach the fifty-foot line to his collar. Since you are making a change, start by working close to the dog, and then *gradually* move away. By next class you should be able to work at ten to fifteen feet and circle your dog. Correct movement out of the Sit with a raised voice. Then go to the puppy and, while praising, *gently* replace him in the Sit on the spot where he was originally placed.

3. CONTINUING THE RECALL: Work this week with the fifty-foot long line if you and your pup are ready. If not, continue to work on the ten-foot line until you are confident.

When working with the fifty-foot line, do not hook it to your waist. Let your puppy *drag* the line as you go for a walk in a distracting situation. Only call your puppy when he is distracted, as this is what must now be reliably learned. Make sure that you are always near the line, and only allow him to move about ten to fifteen feet away from you before stepping on the line to check him, while praising. This will begin to teach him not to range too far from you. If you need to correct your pup for not responding to your Recall signal, pick up the line and jerk *hard*, while praising. If you have a larger puppy, you may want to wear gloves.

4. LIGHT LINE WALKING: If your One-handed Walking is going well, try walking your puppy on the long training line. If you have difficulties, use the ten-foot line, hooked to your waist as a transition. Continue to praise and pat your leg for attention. Step on the line and praise if your puppy gets too far out of position. Continue to challenge your pup's attention by working under distracting conditions and introducing new experiences.

Don't forget to read the instructions on eliminating the food reward.

Eliminating the Food Reward

Food rewards are a useful tool for introducing and reinforcing behaviors, overcoming stress, and as an occasional motivator, but none of us wants to have to go around with a pocket full of doggie treats in order to get our dogs to respond!

As we're sure you've learned, dogs are very clever when it comes to food. If you want to get away from using food all the time *you* also have to be very clever. It's very easy for them to figure out what's going on (no more food), if you're not very, very precise and systematic in the way the food is phased out.

There are two important elements in the process:

1. The food is eliminated *gradually* on a *random* basis so that the dog never knows exactly when he will be rewarded with food.

2. Your actions when you don't give the food reward must be as identical as possible to when you do so the dog is not cued by your behavior whether or not he is to receive a treat. In other words, when you're not giving the treat, pretend that your are!

As you begin to reduce the use of food, simply "forget" to give the treat about 25% of the time. Continue to hold the food in your signal hand and pretend to present it, but instead of actually feeding, your hand should pass the mouth and stroke the side of the head and neck. Continue to praise especially enthusiastically. Remember to offer the food randomly, with no particular pattern.

After about a week increase your "forgetfulness" to 50%. Then gradually phase out the food over a period of weeks until you are using food only occasionally during your regular training routine. This can be gradually phased out too as your puppy performs in many different locations. Food can *always* be used on a 100% reward basis when introducing new commands, new locations, or in particularly stressful situations.

Some Suggestions for Creative Play

Play is a normal and necessary part of puppy development, but certain types of games may interfere with the establishment of a sound relationship between your puppy and his "adopted pack." The encouragement of aggression by excessive wrestling, roughhousing, tug-of-war, or any other activity which encourages the puppy to act dominantly toward you or other family members may be counterproductive during the subordination process. Teasing or any type of game which might cause pain, fear, distrust, or confusion *must always* be avoided. Have a serious discussion with young children regarding appropriate play. Some games which promote a good relationship and can be used for exercise and fun are:

1. RETRIEVING GAMES: (See "Exercise, A Daily Necessity" on page 34 of your *SuperPuppy* book.) Many puppies find the movement of a ball irresistible and will follow and pick one up with only a little encouragement. To encourage this natural tendency, try bouncing the ball against a wall or into a corner. Keep the distance short at first. If a ball doesn't spark his interest use any toy or item that he likes to pick up and carry.

Once your puppy has the idea, you can vary the game. Try teaching him to catch something tossed in the air. Start with a treat. Have your puppy sitting in front of you, and encourage him to "look" as you drop the treat straight down into his mouth. Gradually increase the distance and toss the treat in a high arc, aiming for his nose. Later use a toy or ball.

Another variation is to teach him to find a hidden treat or toy. Start with a treat hidden in your hand. Let him see you hide it. Once he gets the idea of searching and using his nose, make the game more challenging using a variety of toys and hiding places.

"Let's play!"

2. HIDE AND SEEK: This is a two-person game. One person holds the puppy and the other hides. Begin simply so that he can be successful *immediately*. Hide nearby and encourage him to find you by praising enthusiastically when he's released. Give a food reward when he finds you. Gradually make the hiding places more difficult and remain silent until he finds you. Before long he'll be able to find you anywhere!

3. CHASE OR BACK-AND-FORTH RECALLS: (See page 35 of your *SuperPuppy* book.) This requires that he's been taught to come to at least one other person. Start out by having the other person hold him while you go about eight feet away. Tell the person not to release him until you raise your hand. Call him and run back away from him praising, *then* raise your hand. When he gets to you, reward him. Alternate by having your partner call him, too. Gradually increase the distance.

4. FOLLOW THE LEADER: Expand your puppy's horizons by introducing him to new experiences. Gradually teach him to walk anywhere — on stairs, under tables, on strange surfaces. Playground equipment is a great challenge. Use the Three FIB technique to teach him to follow you anywhere! Build confidence with simple obstacles at first, and progress to greater difficulty as he becomes bold and trusting.

CLASS V — "Hit the Deck"

1. INTRODUCTION TO THE DROP: 1) Kneel and shape your puppy into a Sit at your left side or directly in front of you. Place the leash on the ground and step or kneel on it. Do not use a Sit command at this time. 2) Hold a treat in your *right* hand. Your left hand holds the puppy's collar and your forearm rests along his back. 3) Give the command, "(Puppy's name), Drop," while simultaneously sweeping your right hand, *palm down,* toward the ground and away from the puppy's muzzle. Use your left hand and arm to put steady but gentle pressure on the puppy's back and shoulders. Praise *immediately* and continue to praise until the puppy is all the way down. 4) Reward by giving a treat and petting lavishly. 5) Your puppy may get up right way if he wants to.

2. CONTINUING THE WAITS: Don't combine the Drop command with the Wait until you have had one week of practice on the Drop alone *and* your pup is going down readily. We recommend that you focus your practice on the Drop/Wait unless you plan on doing obedience competition where both positions are required. This is because the Drop/Wait is more stable and easier for the pup to maintain for longer periods of time. Gradually increase the time and distance for the Drop/Wait while using the fifty-foot light line. Make sure that your puppy responds to your raised voice as a correction for movement before you increase the distance beyond ten feet. REMEMBER THAT YOU MUST PRACTICE THE WAITS UNDER DISTRACTION, SO GO LOOKING FOR TROUBLE!

Use forearm pressure to prompt the pup down.

3. CONTINUING THE RECALL: Continue to work with the puppy dragging the fifty-foot line. If things are going well, increase the

difficulty by placing your pup in very tempting, distracting situations. If you are having trouble, work with the short line, leash, and/or less difficult situations. REMEMBER, many problems can be solved by returning to earlier stages in training and clearing up confusion. Slower progress that results in success is better than trying to go too fast and winding up with an unreliable, inconsistent Recall.

Reduce the food reinforcement by 25% as described in last week's handout. REMEMBER: In order for your puppy to learn to come reliably at all times, he *must* be worked in different locations under distracting conditions on a *regular basis.*

Next week will be our fun graduation class. This is a "no pressure" evening for you and your pup to work on some new obstacles, show off what you've learned, and receive some tips for further training. Prepare by concentrating on the Drop command, Fronts and Waits *under distraction,* and by reviewing the Four Principles of Training.

CLASS VI —CONTINUING ON

1. CONTINUING THE RECALL: By this time your pup should be coming when called and sitting promptly while dragging the fifty-foot line. Continue to let him drag the line, and, if needed, don't hesitate to give him an occasional refresher course on a shorter line or the six-foot leash.

Continue to work on the recall under challenging, distracting conditions, remembering to call the dog *only once,* and praise immediately while using the hand signal. Correct any hesitation by getting to the line *as fast as you can* and giving it a good jerk. Remember to praise while you're moving for the line and as the pup comes toward you. Continue to phase out food rewards by substituting praise and petting.

When you're sure your puppy will perform properly under many different distracting conditions, phase out the line by cutting it back a little bit at a time. The line should disappear gradually over a two- to three-month period so your pup will never be able to tell exactly how long it is! You may also want to remove the bolt snap and tie the line *securely* to the collar, eliminating one more cue that the line is present.

At the first sign of hesitation, lack of attention, or slowness, attach a fifty-foot line to your dog's collar and jerk it firmly while calling the dog. Do this until you are again getting prompt responses, and then continue to phase out the line. Some dogs will need occasional reminders throughout their lives.

2. CONTINUING THE SIT/WAIT & WAIT WHILE DOWN: By this time your pup should be waiting for a minute on the fifty-foot line while you are twenty feet away. The next step is to eliminate reliance on the line. Drop the training line on the ground, and keep your foot on it. Use your voice to correct movement away from the initial position. Increase your distance in very small increments.

Phase out the line by cutting it back gradually as is done for the Recall. If you need to return to your puppy to reposition him, REMEMBER that you *must* be *very gentle* and praise in a soft, reassuring tone of voice.

A reliable Wait can only be developed when you quickly correct any movement out of the initial position and teach under distracting conditions. Remember that your raised voice must stop any attempt to change position. If you find that this is not so, reteach the Wait from the beginning.

Once your dog is allowed to break a Wait for any reason without being immediately and effectively corrected, you may have a *very* difficult time convincing him to Wait reliably again.

3. CONTINUING THE DROP COMMAND: As your puppy begins to understand and respond readily to the Drop signal, remove your left hand and arm from his back and gradually begin to stand up while giving the Drop signal. As in the recall, the food reward is gradually phased out and replaced with praise and petting.

In teaching *anything* remember to give your pup the opportunity to be successful by: 1) Following the Four Principles of Training — three in a row, start at the end, fast feedback, and incremental teaching; and 2) immediately returning to an earlier stage in teaching if conditions change or problems are encountered. Make sure you also remember to make learning fun!

Don't hesitate to contact us if you have any questions about your dog's training or behavior!

INDEX

B

Barking 23, 25, 26, 30, 32. *See also* Territorial Barking
Beanbag 31, 42–43
Behavior problem. *See* Problem solving
Bond 20, 56
Booby Trapping 47–48
Brushing. *See* Grooming

C

Collar Check 23
Come when called. *See* Recall
Confinement. *See* Den
Controlled Walking 26–29, 36–37
  "Father Time" 36
  Keep-Away 37
  Left-Sided Walking 51
  One-Handed Walking 50
  Quiet Walking 55
  With ten foot line 52

D

Den 14–16, 45–46
Distraction 40, 51, 64, 69, 86, 88, 89, 91, 92, 94, 95
  and fifty foot line 65
  during Waits 55
  on low ramp 71
Drop 72, 73, 94, 96
Drop/Wait. *See* Wait While Down

E

Exercise 30, 82, 93. *See also* Retrieving

F

F. I. B. 58–60
Fast Feedback 18–19, 29, 54, 59, 66, 76, 91, 96
Father Time. *See* Controlled Walking
Food
  and fast feedback 59
  and stress 23
  diet 45
  guarding 85
  lures 61
  reward 27, 34, 39, 40, 58, 71, 86
    after Wait 54, 66, 92
    phasing out 67–68, 69, 73, 77, 92, 95, 96
Front. *See* Recall

G

Graduation 7, 12, 73, 74, 76, 77, 95
Greeting 26. *See also* Socialization
Grooming 38, 44, 56, 85, 87, 89
Group 10, 27, 29, 30, 41, 45
  leaders 10–12

H

Hand signals. *See* descriptions of individual commands
Heeling. *See* Controlled Walking
Homework handouts 81–96

I

Increments 59, 60, 62, 66, 70, 76, 95
  in teaching Waits 55

J

Jump obstacle 74, 75
Jumping up 31, 42, 49

K

K.P.T. 7, 12
Keep-Away. *See* Controlled Walking

L

Leash. *See* Controlled Walking, Recall, Wait
  as training tool 11
  explained at Orientation 21
  use at First Puppy Night 23
Left-Sided Walking. *See* Controlled Walking
Light line 59, 88, 92, 94. *See also* Recall
  Fifty foot 65
  Ten foot 51–52
Listening Position 24–26, 33, 50
Low ramp. *See* Obstacles

O

Obedience 6, 7, 8, 9, 10, 12, 51, 78, 94
Obstacles 11, 16, 17, 69, 94
  at graduation 74–77
  introducing 58, 60
  low ramp 70
  tunnel 61–68
One-Handed. *See* Controlled Walking
One-Handed Walking. *See* Controlled Walking: One-Handed Walking
Orientation 9, 10, 13–22

P

Play. *See* Exercise, Retrieving, Socialization

Problem behavior 50. *See also* Problem solving
Problem solving 12, 41–43
Puppy kindergarten. *See* K.P.T.

R

Ramp. *See* V-ramp
Recall 37–41, 85, 86, 88, 92, 95. *See also* Light line, Tunnel
Release 89, 92
   from Sit/Wait 54
   from Wait while down 66
Retrieving 30, 43, 48, 93

S

Shaker Can 32–33
Shaker can 48
Shaping. *See* descriptions of individual commands
Sit. *See also* Listening Position, Recall, Wait
   at end of Recall 39, 86
   Sit/Wait 53, 54, 55, 89
Skills. *See* descriptions of individual commands
Social development 5
Socialization 7, 16, 23. *See also* Greeting
Stay. *See* Wait
Stimulation 13, 16–17, 46. *See also* Obstacles
Stop Signal 25, 31, 33
Submission. *See* Subordination
Subordination 11, 30, 34, 48, 85, 89, 93
   and Drop 73
   at First Puppy Night 35, 36
     Take-Down 33
   at Second Puppy Night 43–44
   explained at Orientation 13, 19
   vs. fear 20

T

Teeter board 58, 62, 69, 70, 75, 76. *See also* Obstacles
Territorial Barking 32–33. *See also* Shaker Can
Time Out 27, 28, 37, 39, 40, 55, 59, 61, 84, 86
Tunnel 11, 58, 60–64, 69, 70, 74. *See also* Obstacles

V

V-barrier 75, 76. *See also* Obstacles
V-ramp 58, 62, 69, 70, 75. *See also* Obstacles

W

Wait 75, 77, 94, 95
   and V-barrier 76
   on low ramp 71
   Sit/Wait 52–55, 88, 92
   While Down 58, 65–66, 91
Weave poles 75, 76. *See also* Obstacles
Wolf 5, 13–15, 16, 17, 19
   subordination in pack 34